S0-ARC-019

Testicular Cancer

LIFE UNIVERSITY LIBRARY
WILHUHAWN

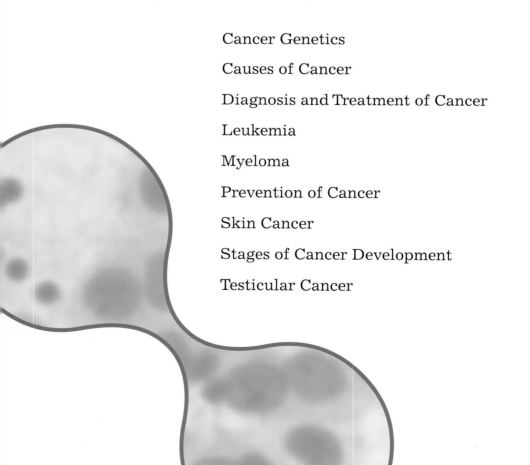

Testicular Cancer

Kathleen M. Verville, Ph.D.

Consulting Editor,
Donna Bozzone, Ph.D.,
Professor of Biology
Saint Michael's College

LIFE UNIVERSITY LIBRARY
1269 BARCLAY CIRCLE
MARIETTA, GA 30060
770-426-2688

CHELSEA HOUSE
PUBLISHERS
An imprint of Infobase Publishing

THE BIOLOGY OF CANCER: TESTICULAR CANCER

Copyright © 2009 by Infobase Publishing, Inc.

All rights reserved. No part of this book may be reproduced or utilized in any form or by any means, electronic or mechanical, including photocopying, recording, or by any information storage or retrieval systems, without permission in writing from the publisher. For information, contact:

Chelsea House
An imprint of Infobase Publishing
132 West 31st Street
New York NY 10001

Library of Congress Cataloging-in-Publication Data
Verville, Kathleen.
  Testicular cancer / Kathleen Verville ; consulting editor, Donna M. Bozzone.
      p. cm. — (Biology of cancer)
  Includes bibliographical references and index.
  ISBN-13: 978-1-60413-166-6 (alk. paper)
  ISBN-10: 1-60413-166-7 (alk. paper)
  1. Testis—Cancer—Popular works. I. Title. II. Series.

  RC280.T4V84 2009
  616.99'463—dc22

                    2008039737

Chelsea House books are available at special discounts when purchased in bulk quantities for businesses, associations, institutions, or sales promotions. Please call our Special Sales Department in New York at (212) 967-8800 or (800) 322-8755.

You can find Chelsea House on the World Wide Web at http://www.chelseahouse.com

Text design by James Scotto-Lavino
Cover design by Ben Peterson
Illustrations by Sholto Ainslie

Printed in the United States of America

Bang EJB 10 9 8 7 6 5 4 3 2 1

This book is printed on acid-free paper.

All links and Web addresses were checked and verified to be correct at the time of publication. Because of the dynamic nature of the Web, some addresses and links may have changed since publication and may no longer be valid.

CONTENTS

◆

FOREWORD

◆

Approximately 1,500 people die each day of cancer in the United States. Worldwide, more than 8 million new cases are diagnosed each year. In affluent, developed nations such as the United States, around 1 out of 3 people will develop cancer in his or her lifetime. As deaths from infection and malnutrition become less prevalent in developing areas of the world, people live longer and cancer incidence increases to become a leading cause of mortality. Clearly, few people are left untouched by this disease, because of either their own illness or that of loved ones. This situation leaves us with many questions: What causes cancer? Can we prevent it? Is there a cure?

Cancer did not originate in the modern world. Evidence of humans afflicted with cancer dates from ancient times. Examinations of bones from skeletons that are more than 3,000 years old reveal structures that appear to be tumors. Records from ancient Egypt, written more than 4,000 years ago, describe breast cancers. Possible cases of bone tumors have been observed in Egyptian mummies that are more than 5,000 years old. It is even possible that our species' ancestors developed cancer. In 1932 Louis Leakey discovered a jawbone from either *Australopithecus* or *Homo erectus*, which possessed what appeared to be a tumor. Cancer specialists examined the jawbone and suggested that the tumor was due to Burkitt's lymphoma, a type of cancer that affects the immune system.

It is likely that cancer has been a concern for the human lineage for at least a million years.

Human beings have been searching for ways to treat and cure cancer since ancient times, but cancer is becoming an even greater problem today. Because life expectancy increased dramatically in the twentieth century because of public health successes such as improvements in our ability to prevent and fight infectious disease, more people live long enough to develop cancer. Children and young adults can develop cancer, but the chance of developing the disease increases as a person ages. Now that so many people live longer, cancer incidence has increased dramatically in the population. As a consequence, the prevalence of cancer came to the forefront as a public health concern by the middle of the twentieth century. In 1971 President Richard Nixon signed the National Cancer Act and thus declared "war" on cancer. The National Cancer Act brought cancer research to the forefront and provided funding and a mandate to spur research to the National Cancer Institute. During the years since that action, research laboratories have made significant progress toward understanding cancer. Surprisingly, the most dramatic insights came from learning how normal cells function, and by comparing that to what goes wrong in cancer cells.

Many people think of cancer as a single disease, but it actually comprises more than 100 different disorders in normal cell and tissue function. Nevertheless, all cancers have one feature in common: All are diseases of uncontrolled cell division. Under normal circumstances, the body regulates the production of new cells very precisely. In cancer cells, particular defects in deoxyribonucleic acid, or DNA, lead to breakdowns in the cell communication and growth control normal in healthy cells. Having escaped these controls, cancer cells can become invasive and spread to other parts of the body. As a consequence, normal tissue and organ functions may be seriously disrupted. Ultimately cancer can be fatal.

Even though cancer is a serious disease, modern research has provided many reasons to feel hopeful about the future of cancer treatment and prevention. First, scientists have learned a great deal about the specific genes involved in cancer. This information paves the way for improved early detection, such as identifying individuals with a genetic predisposition to cancer and monitoring their health to ensure the earliest possible detection. Second, knowledge of both the specific genes involved in cancer and the proteins made by cancer cells has made it possible to develop very specific and effective treatments for certain cancers. For example, childhood leukemia, once almost certainly fatal, now can be treated successfully in the great majority of cases. Similarly, improved understanding of cancer cell proteins led to the development of new anticancer drugs such as Herceptin, which is used to treat certain types of breast tumors. Third, many cancers are preventable. In fact, it is likely that more than 50 percent of cancers would never occur if people avoided smoking, overexposure to sun, a high-fat diet, and a sedentary lifestyle. People have tremendous power to reduce their chances of developing cancer by making good health and lifestyle decisions. Even if treatments become perfect, prevention is still preferable to avoid the anxiety of a diagnosis and the potential pain of treatment.

The books in the Biology of Cancer series reveal information about the causes of the disease; the DNA changes that result in tumor formation; ways to prevent, detect, and treat cancer; and detailed accounts of specific types of cancers that occur in particular tissues or organs. Books in this series describe what happens to cells as they lose growth control and how specific cancers affect the body. The Biology of Cancer also provides insights into the studies undertaken, the research experiments done, and the scientists involved in the development of the present state of knowledge of this disease. In this way, readers get to see beyond "the facts" and understand more about the process of biomedical research. Finally, the books in the Biology of Cancer series provide information to help readers make healthy choices that can reduce the risk of cancer.

Cancer research is at a very exciting crossroads, affording scientists the challenge of scientific problem solving as well as the opportunity to engage in work that is likely to directly benefit people's health and well-being. I hope that the books in this series will help readers learn about cancer. Even more, I hope that these books will capture your interest and awaken your curiosity about cancer so that you ask questions for which scientists presently have no answers. Perhaps some of your questions will inspire you to follow your own path of discovery. If so, I look forward to your joining the community of scientists; after all, there is still a lot of work to be done.

Donna M. Bozzone, Ph.D.
Professor of Biology
Saint Michael's College
Colchester, Vermont

1

YOUNG MEN

KEY POINTS

♦ Testicular cancer can occur at any age, but most cases occur in men in their late teens through thirties.

♦ Most testicular cancers form from cells in the testes known as germ cells. These cells normally produce sperm.

♦ Although testicular cancer is a relatively rare cancer, the number of cases has increased in recent years.

♦ The causes of testicular cancer are not known, but some risk factors for the disease have been recognized.

♦ Advances in the treatment of testicular cancer have helped make testicular cancer one of the most curable types of cancer.

A TYPICAL TESTICULAR CANCER PATIENT

In 1999, third baseman Mike Lowell, 24 years old and recently married, had just been traded to the Florida Marlins from the New York Yankees. During the routine physical examination required of major-league baseball players before the start of the season, Lowell's doctor discovered a problem: One of Lowell's testicles felt as if it contained a **tumor**. The lump had not caused him pain, so Lowell had not noticed it. Because most testicular tumors in men Lowell's age are **malignant tumors** (cancer), the next step was to remove the entire testis, or testicle, in a type of surgery called an **orchiectomy**. To do this, his doctor made a small, shallow incision in Lowell's lower abdomen, just above the crease of his leg. The surgeon then pulled the testicle out from the scrotum, the sac in which the testicles sit, and cut the connections between the testicle and the body. The testicle was then sent to a laboratory, where another physician, a **pathologist**, studied thin slices of it through a microscope. As expected, the look and arrangement of the tumor cells showed that the tumor was malignant; Mike Lowell had testicular cancer.

Once the pathologist determined that the tumor was cancerous, the next step was to determine the type of testicular cancer. This was important because the type of cancer would determine which treatments the doctors would use and how likely Lowell would be to survive. The two main categories of testicular cancer are "germ cell" and "non-germ cell." The pathologist determined that Lowell had a type of testicular cancer called **seminoma**, which belongs to the germ cell category. In a testicular **germ cell cancer**, a **germ cell** in the testis—a cell that normally would have divided to produce sperm—acquires cancer-causing mutations or alterations in its genetic material and divides to produce

Figure 1.1   Mike Lowell, shown here playing for the
Florida Marlins, survived a type of testicular cancer called a
seminoma. *(© CNRI/Photo Researchers, Inc.)*

a malignant tumor. Germ cell cancers are the most common type of testicular cancer.

Because seminomas are sensitive to radiation, Lowell subsequently underwent three weeks of radiation therapy. Radiation therapy exposes cells to a focused beam of high-energy radiation. For testicular cancer it is used to kill any cancer cells that might have **metastasized** to **lymph nodes**. The radiation therapy made him nauseous and tired, yet his illness did not keep him away from baseball for long. By late May of the 1999 season, Lowell was a starting player for the Florida Marlins. In recognition of the courage and perseverance he had shown in overcoming the adversity he had faced, Lowell received baseball's Tony Conigliaro Award. In the years since his cancer diagnosis and treatment, Lowell has been recognized for his undeniable talent with a Rawlings Gold Glove and multiple All-Star appearances, and he and his wife Bertica have had two children.

Mike Lowell is not alone in his struggles with testicular cancer. Although testicular cancer is an uncommon form of cancer, the National Cancer Institute (NCI) estimated that in 2008 there would be 8,090 men in the United States diagnosed with the disease. For reasons that are not yet understood, the annual number of cases of testicular germ cell cancer worldwide has more than doubled since the 1950s.

There are several aspects of Lowell's case that make him a typical testicular cancer patient. Although cancer of any type is a rare diagnosis for a 24-year-old, Lowell's testicular cancer diagnosis came at an age that is typical for the disease. The NCI reports that for the years 2000 to 2004, only 2.7 percent of all cancers occurred in the 20 to 34 age group. However, the numbers are quite different for testicular cancer. Of all of the testicular cancer cases reported, 46.2 percent occurred in individuals who were 20 to 34 years old. An additional 30.3 percent occurred in patients between the ages of 35 and 44 years. Of all the types of cancer diagnosed in men between the ages of 15 and 34, testicular cancer is the most common. Testicular cancer can occur at any age, but is most often a disease of young men—some still in high school, others in college, many just beginning their careers and families.

Lowell's case is also typical because he survived and was able to return to a physically demanding career. The NCI reports that 380 testicular cancer deaths are expected in 2008. While this number is hardly negligible—thanks to important advances in medicine and the remarkable (but still poorly understood) sensitivity of testicular cancer cells to chemotherapy and, at times, radiation—the survival rate for testicular cancer is far better than for most other types of cancer. For some forms of testicular cancer, such as Lowell's, the survival rate is now greater than 99 percent.

It is also not unusual for patients who have survived testicular cancer to conceive children after treatment, which often involves the removal of a testicle as well as radiation treatment that could damage the sperm-producing ability of the remaining testicle. This outcome is particularly important for patients with testicular cancer, because the disease tends to occur before many men have completed—or, in many cases, even contemplated—having a family. Sometimes the man's sperm is collected and stored (banked) before the potentially damaging therapy begins.

DETECTION OF TESTICULAR CANCER

Sometimes, as in Lowell's case, testicular cancer is detected during a routine physical exam. Physicians might discover that a testicle either has a lump in it or is enlarged. However, many physicians do not routinely check male patients for abnormalities of the testicles during routine checkups.

In other cases, the patient may discover a problem. He might notice a lump or a firm area in the testicle, or he may notice that the testicle is enlarged or swollen. Other indications are a feeling of heaviness in the scrotum or pain, tenderness, discomfort, or a dull ache in the testis or scrotum. However, many patients do not experience discomfort.

Lumps and other changes in the testicles are most easily noticed if a man is in the habit of routinely examining himself. A person who notices a problem should see a physician immediately. Sometimes a person is embarrassed to talk about his testicles or afraid of the diagnosis and therefore delays seeking assistance. The American Urological Association reports that the average time span between when a man detects a problem and when it is brought to the attention of a physician is five months. This is problematic because testicular cancer can quickly spread to other parts of the body. Although the cancer can often be effectively treated even after it has spread, the treatment needed at that point may be more intensive and more extensive.

If an abnormal testicle is not noticed or is ignored, the patient may notice symptoms that result from the metastasis of the cancer from the testicle to other areas of the body. If the cancer spreads to certain lymph nodes of the abdomen, the patient may experience pain in the back or the abdomen. Figure skater and Olympic gold medalist Scott Hamilton was diagnosed with testicular cancer in his late thirties. He had pain in his mid-abdomen that was so severe it prevented him from standing up straight. Hamilton had a type of germ cell cancer classified as a **nonseminoma** that had metastasized to lymph nodes in his abdomen. Despite the abdominal metastases, Hamilton was successfully treated with surgeries (one to remove the affected testicle and one to remove abdominal lymph nodes) and chemotherapy. Sean Kimerling, an Emmy Award winning sports anchorman and pregame announcer for the New

York Mets, lost his battle with nonseminoma testicular cancer at the age of 37—just one month following his diagnosis; he had suffered severe back pain from the metastases that he had mistakenly attributed to a physical injury.

Once a problem comes to the attention of a physician, the next step taken is often an **ultrasound** exam. Ultrasound technology uses sound waves to visualize the testis, and can help to rule out other causes as well as evaluate a tumor. Blood tests are also performed to determine whether **alpha-fetoprotein** molecules are present in the blood. Some types of testicular cancer cells can form these and other molecules. Because they can indicate the presence in the body of certain types of cancer cells, these molecules are called **tumor markers**.

The testicle can be easily accessed in its position outside the main body cavity, so one might expect that the next step would be a biopsy in which a small sample of the tumor would be taken by inserting a needle through the scrotum. However, most testicular tumors in pubescent males are malignant and obtaining a tissue sample this way risks spreading the cancer cells, so the next step is usually the removal of the entire testicle, an orchiectomy. After this procedure, the removed testicle is examined in a pathology laboratory.

The pathologist who evaluates the testicle examines the way the tumor appears to the naked eye and the way the cells and tissues of the tumor look under a microscope. The tumor marker information from the blood tests is also considered. The microscopic analysis and tumor marker information allows the pathologist to determine whether the tumor is malignant and, if it is, what type of testicular cancer is present. Although most testicular tumors are germ cell tumors, there are other types to consider. And while germ cell tumors are categorized as seminomas (seminomatous germ cell tumors) or nonseminomas (nonseminomatous germ cell tumors), these two categories actually encompass several different types of tumors. Sometimes germ cell tumors contain several types of cancer cells and are referred to as **mixed germ cell tumors (MGCTs)**. Identifying the exact type of cancer is important because the different types of cancer cells can spread in different ways within the body and respond differently to the available treatments. For example, seminomas typically respond well to radiation therapy, but nonseminomas do not.

TREATMENT OF TESTICULAR CANCER

Removal of the testicle, which is necessary in order to confirm cancer and determine cancer type, is also an important step in the treatment of the cancer. If all of the cancer cells are confined to a tumor in a testicle, then removal of the testicle eliminates the cancer. In cases where the cancer seems confined to the testis, a physician may choose to avoid any follow-up treatment and instead carry out surveillance, carefully and regularly monitoring the patient for any signs of recurrence of the disease. Evidence has shown, however, that between 15 and 20 percent of these surveillance-only patients experience a recurrence of their cancer (relapse), so the decision to use surveillance instead of treatment must be carefully weighed.

Most testicular cancer patients are not good candidates for surveillance. Instead, they undergo additional treatment following the orchiectomy. The cancer treatments that may be performed after the orchiectomy include (a) radiation therapy (the use of radiation to kill cancer cells); (b) **chemotherapy** (the use of chemicals to kill cancer cells); and (c) additional surgery, often to remove affected lymph nodes from the back of the abdominal area.

At the time of the initial diagnosis, as well as during and after treatment, the physician must look for signs of metastasis. This can be done by looking for enlarged lymph nodes or for tumors in different parts of the body using imaging tools such as **X-rays** and **computed tomography (CT) scans**, and with removal and laboratory examination (biopsy) of some lymph nodes. Also, if a patient's cancer cells are the type that produce tumor markers, the physician can determine that cancer cells are still present in the body if the markers are detected in the blood.

RISK FACTORS

It is not yet known what causes testicular cancer, but studies are being conducted that consider a variety of possible factors, including genetic, as in an individual's DNA, as well as environmental sources. Among the environmental factors considered are those to which an individual was exposed while in the womb. Certain circumstances increase the risk of developing testicular cancer; those circumstances are knows as **risk factors**.

It is known that **cryptorchidism**, or hidden testis, is a risk factor for testicular cancer. A person who was born with a testicle that did not descend from the abdomen, where it first developed, to the scrotum—a movement that usually happens when a male fetus is still in the uterus—has a greater risk of developing testicular cancer than someone who was born with both testicles properly descended into the scrotum. Evidence suggests that this risk exists even if surgery is performed to properly position the testis after birth.

There are several other known risk factors: Someone who has had one cancerous testicle removed has a greater than normal chance of developing cancer in his other testicle; a man whose brother or father

◆ SPOTLIGHT ON CANCER SCIENTISTS
LAWRENCE EINHORN, M.D.

Lawrence Einhorn, M.D., has played an important role in making testicular cancer, as he describes it, "a model for a curable **neoplasm** [tumor]."[1] The son of a physician, Einhorn knew by the time he was in high school that he wanted to become a doctor. At that time, he certainly could not have known that his clinical research would help to turn testicular cancer from a disease that killed most patients to one that had a survival rate greater than 90 percent.

Einhorn did his undergraduate work at Indiana University and went to medical school at the University of Iowa. Following his residency, he did more specialized training at Indiana University Medical Center and the M.D. Anderson Cancer Center in Houston, Texas. In 1973, he joined the faculty at Indiana University (IU). His work helped to turn the university into a premier center for testicular cancer research and treatment.

Dr. Einhorn's success at IU began shortly after he joined the faculty. Cisplatin, a chemical that had been formed as an unintentional by-product during an experiment done by Barnett Rosenberg at Michigan State University in the 1960s, had been found to have the ability to kill cancer cells. Dr. Einhorn decided to investigate the effectiveness of cisplatin for testicular cancer patients in a type of research study called a clinical trial. For this trial, he modified an existing chemotherapy treatment by adding cisplatin. The survival of the trial subjects was compared to that of the patients whose treatment did not include cisplatin. The results showed cisplatin to be extremely effective. Cisplatin quickly became a standard drug used in combination with others to treat testicular cancer. Over the years, Einhorn and his colleagues have modified the chemotherapy regime, making it even more effective and less toxic to patients.

Beginning in 1996, Dr. Einhorn, along with Dr. Craig Nichols, led the challenging treatment of cyclist Lance Armstrong, whose testicular cancer had spread to his lungs and brain. Given the type and extent of Armstrong's cancer, his prognosis was poor, but following extensive and individualized treatment by the Indiana group, Armstrong recovered. His seven Tour de France titles were won *after* his treatment for testicular cancer.

Einhorn is now a distinguished professor of medicine and the Lance Armstrong Foundation Chair in Oncology at Indiana University. He continues to successfully treat

Figure 1.2   Lance Armstrong, above, initially had a poor diagnosis for his testicular cancer because it had metastasized into his lungs and brain. Treatments developed by Dr. Lawrence Einhorn not only saved Armstrong's life but avoided diminishing his lung capacity in the chemotherapy process, which allowed Armstrong to go on to win seven Tour de France races after his treatment. (© *AP Images*)

(continues)

SPOTLIGHT ON CANCER SCIENTISTS
(continued)

testicular cancer patients and conduct research on the disease. Some of his recent work involves treating patients, whose testicular cancer has responded poorly to existing treatments with very high doses of chemotherapy agents followed by infusion of their own blood-making stem cells to replace those killed during chemotherapy.

had testicular cancer is at increased risk for developing testicular cancer; and testicular cancer affects men of some ethnicities more than others and men in some parts of the world more than in others.

Of course, many men who have a risk factor for testicular cancer do not develop the disease, and many of those who develop testicular cancer do not fall into one of the groups that has a higher than normal risk. There is much to be learned about the causes of testicular cancer and the reasons that some individuals are more likely than others to develop the disease.

IMPORTANT QUESTIONS

Despite the many successes in the treatment of testicular cancer, many scientific and medical questions remain. Perhaps the most pressing medical problem is that, despite remarkable advances in the treatment of testicular cancer, some patients' cancers still do not respond to standard chemotherapy. Researchers want to find ways to help all testicular cancer patients survive.

Another problem is that some of the treatments used are harmful to healthy cells of the body and may therefore cause health problems later in a patient's life. While this is a problem faced in the treatment of all cancers, it is of particular concern for testicular cancer patients, because they are generally quite young at the time of treatment. Scientists want to find ways to reduce the toxicity of the treatments without compromising the excellent success rate.

Epidemiologists and other disease researchers want to understand more fully the causes of testicular cancer. They certainly want to know why the annual number of testicular cases has doubled since the 1950s. Once the causes are known, then there is a chance that testicular cancer can be prevented.

What occurs at the cellular level to cause testicular cancer? Researchers want to know much more about what events happen to the DNA and other molecules in testis cells to cause them to grow and form malignant tumors. They also want to increase their understanding of the unique structure, function, and behavior of the various types of testicular cancer cells.

SUMMARY

The incidence of testicular cancer has increased in recent decades; currently, it affects approximately 8,000 males in the United States each year. Unlike most cancers, it occurs most commonly in young men, usually those in their late teens, twenties, and thirties. It is the most common type of cancer in men between the ages of 15 and 34. Most testicular cancers are germ cell cancers, meaning that they affect cells from the testes that would divide to produce sperm. The causes of testicular cancer are not known, but there are risk factors, such as being born with an undescended testicle. As a result of scientific and medical advances in recent decades, especially the discovery of the sensitivity of testicular cancer cells to the chemotherapeutic agent cisplatin, testicular cancer—which once killed a high percentage of its patients—has one of the highest survival rates of all cancers.

2

DETECTION OF TESTICULAR CANCER

KEY POINTS

- Early detection of testicular cancer is important for increasing survival and decreasing the treatment needed.

- Males are not routinely screened for testicular cancer by their doctors.

- Awareness of the symptoms of testicular cancer and testicular self-exams can lead to early detection of testicular cancer.

- There are many symptoms of testicular cancer. Most commonly, there is a change in the size, shape, or texture of the testicle. Other symptoms may be noted in the scrotum or areas of the body far from the testes. In some cases, breast tissue may become enlarged.

- The symptom(s) that are experienced by a particular patient vary with the type of testicular cancer and the extent and location of its spread.

JASON: DELAYED DETECTION OF TESTICULAR CANCER

Jason Struble was an 18-year-old student at Lafayette High School in Missouri. He was enjoying his senior year, looking forward to college, and playing varsity basketball. During a late-season game, Jason had some trouble catching his breath; by the next day, his shortness of breath had worsened. A medical exam that evening had the doctors confused as to the source of Jason's symptom until a call to his pediatrician, who suggested they check Jason's testicles for signs of cancer. It did not take the medical team long to complete tests that confirmed the pediatrician's suspicion. At the time of Jason's diagnosis, his cancer was advanced; it had spread from his right testicle to his lungs—the cause of his shortness of breath—and to his abdomen.

Jason's doctors were not the first to notice the enlarged testicle. A few months earlier, Jason had noticed it himself, but he had read that one testicle could be larger than another. Perhaps because the enlarged testicle was not painful, perhaps because he was uncomfortable talking about what he had noticed, or perhaps because he was young and seemingly healthy, he had not mentioned the abnormality to anyone. His father tried to understand Jason's reticence: "I don't know if it was out of ignorance or embarrassment or both that he didn't say anything."[1] Had Jason recognized his enlarged testicle as a sign of testicular cancer and appreciated the urgency of rapid diagnosis and treatment, his outcome most likely would have been different. Twenty-seven months after his diagnosis, Jason Struble lost his battle with testicular cancer.

Jason's silence about his changed testicle is not an unusual behavior in testicular cancer patients. NBC chief legal correspondent Dan Abrams, a testicular cancer survivor, emphasized this problem in a *Today* interview, noting that the average time span from when a person notices an abnormality to diagnosis is six months.[2] There are several reasons that men delay getting a medical opinion. Some hope the problem will go away with time, some are embarrassed to mention the problem because it affects a part of the body associated with sexual reproduction, and most are unaware that they have an early symptom of testicular cancer that requires fast medical attention. Because it is young men who are at greatest risk for testicular cancer, it is especially important for them—and also for those in whom they might confide, such as parents, coaches, friends, and partners—to be aware of the symptoms of testicular cancer and the importance of early detection. Jason learned too late, but he urged his parents to help educate middle school and high school boys about testicular cancer. They have worked to fulfill his wish through the activities of the Jason A. Struble Memorial Cancer Fund, Inc.

DETECTION OF TESTICULAR CANCER: THE ROLES OF THE PHYSICIAN AND PATIENT

It is essential for individuals to check for any testicular abnormality and to bring it to the attention of a physician. It is not enough to rely on routine physical exams for initial detection of the problem. Some physicians do not conduct a testicular exam as a regular part of the physical. Jason's father addresses this on his organization's Web site, reporting that in the six months leading up to the diagnosis, Jason had three physical exams, none of which included a testicular exam. "During physical examinations we have all been asked to turn our heads and cough for a hernia examination, but how many young men have ever been checked or even told about testicular cancer? At 61 years of age I can say for myself—never!"[3]

The American Cancer Society reports that most physicians think that testicular exams should be a part of a physical. However, they are not

Figure 2.1   Jason Struble, shown here in his varsity basketball uniform, remained positive throughout his two-year battle with testicular cancer. His family continues his wish to raise awareness among young men about the importance of self-screening in the early detection of testicular cancer. *(Courtesy of the Jason A. Struble Memorial Cancer Fund, Inc.)*

considered routine to the same degree as other tests, such as listening to the heart. Certainly, a physician cannot check for every disease during a physical. Whether a physician should perform regular testicular exams is a subject of debate, but there is clear consensus that routine testicular cancer screening is unnecessary. There is another—and ultimately a more important—reason not to rely on a physical exam for testicular cancer detection. Even if all physicians were to routinely conduct testicular exams, most cases of testicular cancer would be detected earlier by patient self-examination. Early detection can increase the chance of survival and may decrease the need for additional treatment, such as surgery to remove affected lymph nodes from the back of the abdomen, and the person in the best position to initially suspect a problem is not the physician but the patient himself.

The patient cannot help himself, however, if he is not knowledgeable about testicular cancer. Awareness of the typical ages for testicular cancer, the symptoms of testicular cancer, and the importance of quickly bringing a symptom to the attention of a physician is crucial. But awareness may not be enough. Monthly testicular self-exams are advocated by many, including testicular cancer awareness groups and many health care providers. Even if testicular self-exams are not performed on a regular basis, occasional exams will familiarize a man with the size, shape, and feel of his normal testicles, and this increases the chance that an abnormality will be noticed early.

THE TESTICULAR SELF-EXAM AND THE SYMPTOMS IT CAN DETECT

In humans and some other animals, the testicles are suspended outside of the abdominal cavity in a sac called the scrotum. As a result, early signs of testicular cancer—such as a lump on a testicle or an abnormality in its size or texture—can be easily noticed.

The testicular self-exam is best carried out during or following a warm bath or shower, so that the scrotum is relaxed, which makes it easier to feel the testicle inside. Each testicle should be examined individually using both hands. The thumbs should be placed on the front of the testicle and the index and middle fingers placed behind. Using slight pressure, the testicle should be gently rolled so all surfaces can be felt. If this is done in front of a mirror, any swelling of the

---

◆ SCREENING FOR TESTICULAR CANCER

Why are all males not routinely screened for testicular cancer? The National Cancer Institute defines screening as checking for a disease when there are no symptoms present. For testicular cancer, a screen might involve a physician performing testicular exams, imaging techniques such as ultrasound, and blood tests to look for proteins the presence or concentration of which may indicate testicular cancer. At first, this might seem like an excellent idea, as screening would certainly find cases of testicular cancer. But there is a downside. For any screening test, a comparison of the positives (finding disease early) to the negatives (the consequences of thinking there is disease when there is not) must be made; this is known as an analysis of the risk-benefit ratio. If the benefits outweigh the risks, screening is used. If the risks outweigh the benefits, no screening is performed.

In the case of testicular cancer, a large number of people would have to be screened to catch relatively few cases of cancer. Those few cases

scrotum can also be noted. The exam takes a few minutes to perform carefully.

What does a normal testicle feel like? The testis is egg-shaped and firm, and its surface is smooth. The area along the back of each testicle, however, will not feel smooth. This is where the epididymis, a cord that carries sperm, can be felt. Testicular size varies among individuals, and it is normal for one testicle to be larger than the other. A muscle enables the testicle to be positioned at different locations in the scrotum; at a warm temperature the testicles will probably be low in the scrotum (far

would be the benefit. But what are the risks of extensive screening? Since screening tests are not perfectly accurate there would be some false positive results, meaning that some people would receive a result that suggests they have cancer when they actually do not. In addition to the extreme anxiety that a false positive can cause, additional tests would be required to rule out cancer. The discomfort and possible medical complications caused by follow-up tests are a negative factor, and these tests also take a lot of time and money.

The number of people who would experience a false positive and undergo additional testing is considered to be too high compared to the number of cases of testicular cancer that a physician would detect through routine screening. Therefore, the risks are thought to outweigh the benefits. The high risk-benefit ratio, coupled with the relative effectiveness of treatments and the lack of a study showing that screening decreases mortality, is why the National Cancer Institute and the American Cancer Society do not recommend testicular cancer screening.

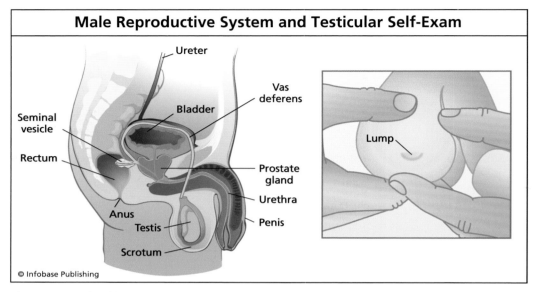

Male Reproductive System and Testicular Self-Exam

© Infobase Publishing

Figure 2.2   The illustration on the left shows a cross section of the male reproductive system. On the right is an illustration showing the recommended technique for performing a testicular self-exam.

from the abdomen). It is normal for one testicle to hang slightly lower in the scrotum than the other.

What testicular cancer symptoms can be detected through a testicular self-exam? Any lump that can be felt on the testicle, even one as small as a grain of rice, is suspicious. Such a lump will usually appear on the side or front of the testicle and will be painless. Any size change (enlargement *or* shrinkage) or hardening of the testicle is also suspicious. Changes are generally noticed in relation to a previous exam, but can also be detected by comparison to the other testicle. The only exception to this is the rare simultaneous occurrence of cancer in both testicles.

OTHER SYMPTOMS OF TESTICULAR CANCER

In addition to lumps and size or texture changes that can be noted from feeling the testicle, other symptoms of testicular cancer include pain or discomfort in the testicle or the scrotum, a feeling of heaviness in the scrotum, or sudden collection of blood or other fluid in the scrotum.

Sometimes testicular cancer causes symptoms outside of the testicle/scrotum. An ache in the groin—the part of the body where the leg connects to the abdomen—or in the lower part of the abdomen may also signal testicular cancer. Some forms of testicular cancer cause breast tissue to become enlarged or tender. In advanced cases, when the cancer has spread to lymph nodes in the back of the abdomen, pain—often severe—can be felt in the lower back. If it has spread to the lungs, the patient can have shortness of breath and chest pain and may cough up blood.

SYMPTOMS OF TESTICULAR CANCER
VARY FROM PATIENT TO PATIENT

There are many possible symptoms of testicular cancer, but most cases of testicular cancer can be noted initially by a change in a testicle or the area around it. Some testicular cancer patients initially experience only a single symptom, while others have more than one symptom. The symptoms experienced vary with the type of testicular cancer and, if it has spread, with the extent and location(s) of metastasis. Therefore, any of the symptoms described could indicate testicular cancer and therefore should quickly be brought to the attention of a physician.

◆ TESTICULAR PROBLEMS OTHER THAN CANCER

Some testicular abnormalities, such as **hydroceles, varicoceles, spermatoceles, epididymitis, orchitis**, and **testicular torsion** have some symptoms in common with testicular cancer. Only a medical evaluation can distinguish testicular cancer from these abnormalities.

A **hydrocele** is fluid accumulation in a sac that surrounds the testicle. It causes the scrotum to swell. Common in newborns, it can occur at any age, and is generally harmless.

A **varicocele** is an enlargement of the veins that carry blood away from the testis. This happens because valves in the veins, which help to prevent blood from backing up as it leaves the testicle, sometimes do not work perfectly, causing blood to pool and the veins to swell. These swollen vessels may feel like spaghetti, and can cause discomfort in the testicle or scrotum. Varicocele develops around puberty in about 15 percent of men. It is similar to the swollen varicose veins you might notice on an older person's leg and is generally harmless.

A **spermatocele** is a fluid-filled cyst in the epididymis. It is common, occurring in about 30 percent of men, and generally harmless.

Epididymitis is an inflammation of the epididymis, usually due to infection. Symptoms can include scrotal pain and swelling, fever, chills, nausea, painful urination, and a frequent urge to urinate.

Orchitis is an inflammation of the testis due to infection. Symptoms include testicular pain and swelling, fever, chills, and nausea.

Testicular torsion is a twisting of the testicle in the scrotum, which crimps the blood supply and other connections in the **spermatic cord** that connects the testis to the abdomen. Symptoms include sudden, severe scrotal pain and scrotal swelling. Urgent medical attention is needed.

SUMMARY

Early detection of testicular cancer increases the chance of survival and may decrease the extent to which further treatments, such as surgery to remove abdominal lymph nodes, are necessary. While testicular cancer might be found during a routine doctor's visit, most cases of testicular cancer are first noticed by the patient. Testicular self-exams and awareness of symptoms can help to detect testicular cancer early. A common early symptom of testicular cancer is a change in the shape, size, or texture of a testicle. Other symptoms may include pain or discomfort in a testicle or the scrotum, fluid accumulation in the scrotum, and pain in areas such as the groin, the abdomen, the back, and the chest. In some cases, a patient may experience shortness of breath, cough up blood, or have enlarged breast tissue. The specific symptoms vary with the type of testicular cancer and whether, and to where, it has spread.

3

DIAGNOSIS OF TESTICULAR CANCER

KEY POINTS

- Diagnosis of testicular cancer is a multistep process that involves ultrasound imaging, blood tests, surgical removal of the testicle, and analysis of testicular tissue in the laboratory.

- Ultrasound is used to determine details of the testicular mass, such as size, location, and whether it is solid.

- Blood tests are performed to look for certain tumor markers that may be present in some types of testicular cancer.

- Testicular tissue removed in surgery is analyzed in the pathology lab.

STEPS TO A DIAGNOSIS

Once a physician suspects testicular cancer, the next step is to confirm the suspicion with a diagnosis. The first step in the diagnosis of testicular cancer is a testicular exam performed by a physician. If the physician feels a mass in the testicle that could be a tumor, the patient will be asked to undergo an imaging procedure known as an ultrasound, which can provide information about the location and composition of the mass. If the ultrasound shows a tumor inside the testis, the most likely diagnosis is testicular cancer. Laboratory analysis of the tumor cells, however, is required for confirmation. While a sample of these cells could theoretically be pulled into a needle inserted through the scrotum, sampling a malignant testicular tumor in this way can risk spreading the cancer to areas where it would not normally spread. The next step, therefore, is surgical removal of the entire testicle, which is then examined in the lab to determine the characteristics of the tumor and the cells of which it is made. (Since most testicular tumors are malignant, there are thankfully very few cases in which a testicle is removed unnecessarily.) This tumor analysis is aided by a blood workup, which is performed before surgery to detect the presence of molecules that are produced in some types of testicular cancer.

ULTRASOUND

An ultrasound is a test that uses sound waves to form images of soft body tissues. The technique is familiar to many people as the method used to view a fetus in utero, or in the uterus. Ultrasound is relatively inexpensive and there is no radiation involved.

A small handheld instrument called a transducer produces high frequency sounds as it passes back and forth over the structures to be studied, in this case the testis and surrounding tissues in the scrotum. A gel is applied to the transducer to help make a good connection between the instrument and the body. When the sound waves hit body structures, they bounce back, or echo. These echoes are then picked up by the transducer and sent to a computer, which converts the sounds into images. Different tissues produce different echoes, and the combination of these echoes produces a meaningful image. The ultrasound technician captures the best images, which are then evaluated by a **radiologist**, a specialist who analyzes medical images.

A testicular tumor will produce different echoes than the surrounding healthy testicular tissue and will therefore stand out against a background of normal tissue. Many testicular tumors produce weaker echoes than healthy tissue, and therefore appear lighter than their surroundings.

In addition to showing the size of the mass, ultrasound allows the assessment of two features that are key to a cancer diagnosis: (1) whether the mass is within the testis (intratesticular) or outside of it (extratesticular), and (2) whether it is a mass of cells (solid) or a sac filled with fluid or semisolid material (cystic). If the mass is extratesticular and cystic, it is almost always benign (not cancerous). Most extratesticular solid masses and intratesticular cystic masses are benign, but a testicular mass that is intratesticular and solid is usually malignant. Therefore, if a testicular ultrasound shows that a mass is within the testicle and solid, the next step will almost certainly be removal of the testicle for laboratory analysis of the tumor.

TUMOR MARKERS IN THE BLOOD

In addition to having an ultrasound to evaluate a testicular mass, the patient will visit a lab to have blood drawn so it can be analyzed for the presence of tumor markers. These are molecules produced by certain cancer cells that can be detected in bodily fluids. Removal of the testicle

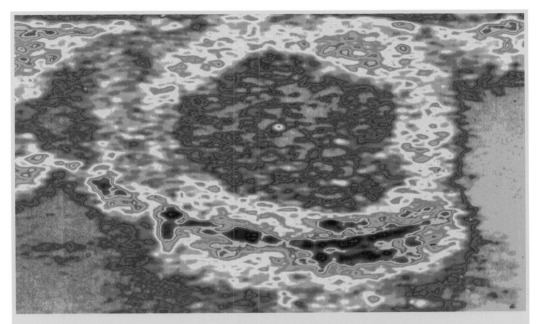

Figure 3.1 This colored ultrasound shows a testicular tumor (blue). Ultrasound images are made by the varying reflections of high-frequency sound waves. Cancerous tissue reflects these waves differently than noncancerous tissue. (© *Mehau Kulyk / Photo Researchers, Inc.*)

will generally cause the concentration of any tumor marker to decrease, so this blood work must be done before surgery. Because some testicular cancers do not produce a tumor marker and tumor marker concentration may be low in the early stages of testicular cancer, the absence of a tumor marker does not rule out testicular cancer. Conversely, because some cells that are not testicular cancer cells can also produce these molecules, the presence of a testicular cancer tumor marker does not confirm testicular cancer. Nonetheless, the presence—and concentration—of one or more of these markers can aid in making a diagnosis of testicular cancer. The type of tumor marker found, or the absence of a tumor marker, is also important in determining the type of testicular cancer (an essential part of the diagnosis). If a tumor marker is found, its concentration indicates the degree to which the disease has advanced. Later, tumor marker concentration can also be used to monitor treatment success. The tumor markers for testicular cancer are alpha-fetoprotein, human chorionic gonadotropin, and lactate dehydrogenase.

Alpha-Fetoprotein

Alpha-fetoprotein (AFP) is a protein normally produced by an embryo (the developmental stage that encompasses the first eight weeks of pregnancy) and, later, the fetus (the developmental stage after the eighth week of pregnancy). The protein is first produced by cells of the **yolk sac**, a sac attached to the embryo that produces the first blood cells as well as the cells that will eventually develop into **gametes** (cells that unite during sexual reproduction, *sperm* in males and *ova* in females). Later in development, AFP is produced by liver cells of the fetus. Scientists are not sure of the function of AFP in the developing baby. After the first trimester of pregnancy, the AFP concentration in the fetal blood begins to decrease, and this decrease continues during the first year of a child's life. From the age of about 8 to 12 months through adulthood, AFP concentrations in the blood are normally low. Like its role in the developing embryo or fetus, the role of AFP in adults—if there is one—is unknown.

Many people are familiar with AFP because of its role as a marker for some birth defects. AFP of developing embryos or fetuses crosses the placenta and enters the mother's circulation. An AFP concentration in the mother's blood that is too high may indicate a problem with the development of the spinal cord; a concentration that is too low may indicate Down syndrome, a chromosome disorder.

Although all individuals have small amounts of AFP in their blood serum, in some diseases, such as liver disease and some cancers, AFP concentrations become elevated. Among the few cancers that cause AFP to rise are some forms of testicular cancer. Testicular cancer can occur at any age, and so doctors who are working with a testicular cancer patient who is younger than one year must remember that an elevated AFP concentration is normal in this age group.

Human Chorionic Gonadotropin

Human chorionic gonadotropin (hCG) is a protein that is made by cells of the developing embryo that are known as **trophoblasts**, and later by cells that develop from trophoblasts: **cytotrophoblasts** and **syncytiotrophoblasts**. These cells are part of an embryo-associated membrane known as the **chorion**, which forms the fetal part of the **placenta**. The placenta is the structure made of both fetal and maternal tissue that allows materials to pass between maternal and fetal blood.

Unlike AFP, the function of hCG is known. hCG interacts with a mother's ovaries to prevent a hormone concentration change that would result in menstruation and loss of the pregnancy. Pregnancy tests are designed to detect the presence of hCG in a woman's urine or blood.

hCG is made of two separate chains, or subunits, an alpha subunit and a beta subunit. The alpha subunit is not unique to hCG, but the beta subunit only occurs in the molecule hCG. Therefore, to detect hCG, scientists look for the beta subunit, or ß-hCG.

hCG is not normally found in the blood serum of males. Its concentration can become elevated in certain diseases, including certain types of testicular cancer. The production of hCG by certain testicular cancers is one reason why some testicular cancers cause enlargement of breast tissue, a condition known as **gynecomastia**.

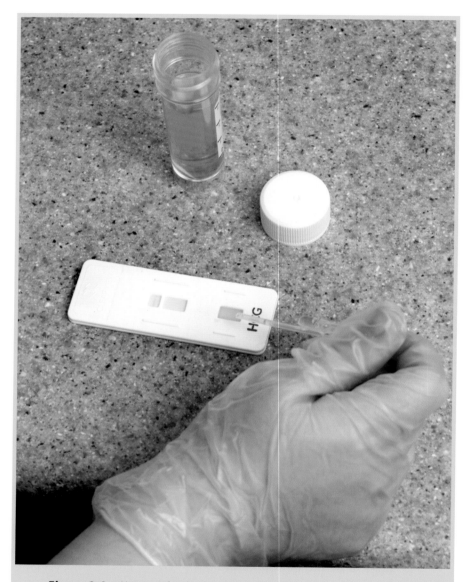

Figure 3.2   Human chorionic gonadotropin (hCG) is a protein released by pregnant women and pregnancy tests, such as the one shown here, use the presence of hCG in the urine or blood serum to detect pregnancy. The presence of this protein in men is a sign of disease, often testicular cancer. *(© Jim Varney/Photo Researchers, Inc.)*

LACTATE DEHYDROGENASE

Lactate dehydrogenase (LDH) is a protein that is normally made by most cells of the body. This protein functions as an **enzyme,** which is a protein that speeds up a particular chemical reaction. LDH is involved in the process by which body cells produce energy from foods. Therefore, the presence of this enzyme in the blood is normal. Its concentration, however, can be elevated when tissue is damaged (for example following a heart attack or in certain diseases, such as liver disease) and in many types of cancers, including some testicular cancers.

THE ORCHIECTOMY AND ANALYSIS

Often, one or both testes are surgically removed in order to evaluate the tissue. The procedure is called a radical inguinal orchiectomy. To perform an orchiectomy, a small, shallow incision is made in an area of the lower abdomen known as the inguinal region. This exposes the spermatic cord, which connects the testicle to important structures in the abdomen. The testicle is pulled up from the scrotum into the incision area. The spermatic cord is then tied and cut. The testicle is then analyzed by a pathologist.

HISTOLOGY

Testicular tumors are classified by the pathologist largely by gross appearance (what the tumor looks like with the naked eye) and by **histology** (what the tumor cells, and the tissue[s] into which those cells are organized, look like when the tumor is sliced, stained, and viewed under a microscope).

Pieces of a tumor are thinly sliced and placed on a microscope slide. Because testicular tumors can be made of more than one cell type, pathologists have to systematically examine tissue from different areas of the tumor to be sure that it has been thoroughly analyzed. The slices are stained with a general tissue stain, usually hematoxylin-eosin. Stains enable the cells—which would not normally stand out from the clear background of the microscope slide—to pick up color so they can be seen. In a hematoxylin-eosin stain, the cells are first stained with a blue dye (hematoxylin) and then with a red dye (eosin). The two dyes differ chemically, and therefore bind differently to separate cell parts. For example, the nucleus becomes stained a bluish purple color by the hematoxylin, while the cytoplasm becomes stained pink by the eosin. Pathologists are well trained in how normal—and ab-normal—testicular cells and tissues stained by hematoxylin-eosin look under a microscope.

As researchers have become aware of specific molecules that are present in some cell types but absent in others, pathologists have been able to use a newer histology method—**immunohistochemistry**—that uses chemicals that specifically stain, or label, the many copies of a particular molecule in a cell. Only cells with that particular molecule are stained, and the stain occurs in the parts of the cell where those molecules are located. This technique is especially useful for pathologists in evaluating tumors, because cancer cells can often be identified by the molecules they have (as well as the molecules they lack).

The staining specificity for immunohistochemistry can be achieved by looking for the molecule in question with a type of molecule known as an **antibody**. Antibodies are proteins that normally play a part in the immune (defense) system by binding to molecules on cells and viruses that are not normally found in the body, triggering complex reactions that help to destroy them. The body has many thousands of different antibodies, and each antibody type is remarkably specific. For example, an antibody that can bind to a molecule unique to the measles virus will not be able to bind to a molecule unique to the chicken pox virus. The *immuno* in *immunohistochemistry* refers to antibodies used to probe for the molecule in question, *histo* refers to the histology technique, and *chemistry* acknowledges the chemical nature of the molecules and their interactions in the test.

For immunohistochemistry, scientists use lab animals, such as mice, to produce antibodies that will bind exclusively to the copies of a specific molecule they want to be able to look for in a cell. Instead of staining the tissue slices with a stain such as hematoxylin-eosin that will dye most parts of the cell, the tissue slices will be coated with a solution containing these antibody molecules. The antibodies will stick to the tissue only if the tissue contains the appropriate molecule.

The cell molecules may have antibodies attached to them, but there is no way to know this because the attached antibodies cannot be seen. Making the antibodies visible can be accomplished in several ways. In the simplest method, before the antibody is added to the tissue slices it is modified by attaching (conjugating) an enzyme to it. Once an antibody-enzyme has been allowed to attach to the cells, the tissue is treated with a molecule that the enzyme can break down. It is the breakdown product of this molecule that acts as a dye. As a result, dye is only deposited on cells near the molecule in question.

SUMMARY

The diagnosis of testicular cancer is a multistep process. Once a physician suspects testicular cancer, the next steps involve analyzing the testicular mass through ultrasound and the blood for tumor markers (AFP, hCG, and LDH) that are made by some types of testicular cancer cells.

If an ultrasound determines that the mass is solid as well as inside the testicle, the tumor is mostly likely malignant. Once this is determined, the next step is removal of the entire testicle and attached spermatic cord in a surgery known as a radical inguinal orchiectomy. The testicle is then sent to a pathologist where it is analyzed. These procedures will not only confirm a testicular cancer diagnosis, but will determine the type of testicular cancer a patient has.

4
THE TESTES

KEY POINTS

- Testes develop in the fetus, in the abdominal cavity. They later move into the scrotum.

- After movement into the scrotum, the testes retain their connections to the abdominal cavity through the spermatic cord. Blood, tissue fluid, and sperm move in tubes through the spermatic cords.

- Testes contain many cells, including testosterone-making Leydig cells, Sertoli cells that assist in sperm production, and cells in the process of becoming sperm.

- Connective tissue covers each testis and divides it into sections that each contain seminiferous tubules separated by the interstitium. Leydig cells are found in the interstitium; Sertoli cells and germ cells are in the seminiferous tubules.

- Seminiferous tubules produce sperm in a stepwise process.

A DOCTOR'S EXPLANATION

During a presurgical meeting with a man suspected of having testicular cancer, the doctor explains that a confirmed diagnosis, as well as determination of the type of testicular cancer, will require laboratory evaluation of the testicle following orchiectomy. The patient is also advised about the different types of testicular cancer, either germ cell cancer, the most common type, or **non–germ cell cancer**. The latter is formed when cells that are not germ cells, such as **Sertoli** and **Leydig** cells, develop into cancer cells and form tumors.

The physician also talks with the patient about the possibility that his cancer has metastasized to parts of his body outside of the testicle. Most testicular cancers that spread from their site of origin do so by way of the lymphatic system to lymph nodes, most commonly those that are located in an area at the back of the abdomen known as the retroperitoneum. The physician might also mention that some cases of testicular cancer spread by way of the circulatory system.

Understanding the anatomy and workings of the testes, as well as the circulatory and lymphatic systems to which they connect, is essential in order to grasp the complexities of testicular cancer.

THE TESTES, THE SCROTUM, AND THE INGUINAL CANAL

The testes are the male reproductive glands, or **gonads**. They are key structures in sexual reproduction. These paired, egg-shaped organs produce spermatozoa, commonly known as sperm. Each of these male gametes has the ability to fertilize a female gamete (egg cell, ovum) to create a zygote, the first cell of the offspring. Testes also produce certain **hormones**, which are chemicals made by cells that travel through blood to affect the function of other cells. The testes are also referred to as male sex glands. The term *gland* implies that these organs secrete materials. Testes are **exocrine glands**, which means that they secrete materials (in this case sperm) through a duct to the outside of the body. They are also **endocrine glands,** because they secrete materials (hormones) directly into the bloodstream.

Each testis is suspended by its spermatic cord in the scrotum (scrotal sac), a skin-covered sac that lies just below the abdomen and behind the penis. Each also has a piece of tissue—the **gubernaculum**—that connects it to the inside of the scrotum. A male's scrotum is formed in utero at the fetal stage from tissues of the lower abdomen. These tissues expand to form a pocket-like extension of the abdominal cavity, which becomes the scrotum.

The fetal scrotum is connected to the abdominal cavity by tissues that are arranged to form two tubelike passageways known as the **inguinal canals**. These connections play an essential role in development: The testes of the fetus develop at the back of the abdominal cavity near the kidneys, outside of (and behind) a membrane that lines much of the abdominal cavity, known as the **peritoneum.** This area is known as the **retroperitoneum**. To move from their location in this retroperitoneal space to the scrotum, the testes must pass through the inguinal canals. The descent of each testis into the scrotum normally occurs before birth. Each testis moves from the retroperitoneum, through the abdominal opening of the inguinal canal (the **internal inguinal ring**), through the inguinal canal, and out the scrotal opening of that inguinal canal (the **external inguinal ring**) to the scrotum. Connective tissue then closes the inguinal canal, separating the abdominal cavity from the scrotum.

Although closure of the inguinal canal prevents materials from moving freely between the abdominal cavity and the scrotum, connections between the two areas of the body must be maintained. With regard to the testes, the following connections are necessary: (1) blood must be able to flow back and forth between the abdominal cavity and the testes; (2) sperm made in the testes must be able to travel to the abdominal cavity where it enters the **urethra**, a tube that carries it from the body during ejaculation; and (3) excess **tissue fluid** of the testes, which originates from the fluid part of the blood in the circulatory system, must be able to travel to the abdominal cavity on its journey back to the circulatory system. The connections between the testes and the abdominal cavity of the body are made by blood vessels, **lymph vessels** (the tissue fluid-carrying tubes of the lymphatic system), and the **vas deferens**, a sperm-carrying duct. These tubes are tethered together by muscle and connective tissue in a structure known as the spermatic cord, which carries these tubes through the connective tissue of the inguinal canal. Nerves also run between the abdomen and the testes through the spermatic cord. The spermatic cord thus does much more than suspend the testes in the scrotum: It allows for the testes to connect to essential structures in the abdominal cavity. The spermatic cord is also the conduit for testicular cancer cells to move from the testes to the abdomen and, at times, beyond the abdomen to other body areas.

THE ANATOMY OF THE TESTIS

The surface of the testis (Figure 4.1) is smooth, except for an area known as the **hilus**, where the blood vessels, lymph vessels, and sperm-carrying ducts connect. The smooth surface is created largely by the testis' main covering, the **tunica albuginea.** This tough, fibrous layer of connective tissue (supportive tissue made primarily of the protein collagen) contains embedded muscle cells.

In the area of the hilus, the tunica albuginea penetrates to the inside of the testis, forming an area rich in connective tissue known as the **mediastinum testis**. Strands of connective tissue fan out from the **mediastinum** across the testis to the inside of the tunica albuginea. These provide structural support and divide the inside of the testis into regions known as **lobules**. It is estimated that there are about 250 lobules per testis.

To the outside (scrotal side) of the tunica albuginea is another covering, the **tunica vaginalis**, a flattened sac with two layers that wrap around much of the testis. The tunica vaginalis partially covers but does not penetrate the testis. This closed sac is actually a remnant of a section of the peritoneum that moves into the scrotum during fetal development. (Recall that a condition known as hydrocele can cause scrotal swelling. In hydroceles, it is the tunica vaginalis that fills with fluid.)

Each testis lobule contains one to about four sperm-producing tubules known as **seminiferous tubules**. These are separated by the **interstitium**, an area of connective tissue with embedded cells: defense cells, connective-tissue making cells, and hormone-producing Leydig cells. **Testosterone**, the predominant hormone made by the Leydig cell, is required for many aspects of male development (especially during fetal development and puberty) and function, including sperm production by the seminiferous tubules. The seminiferous tubules make up approximately 70 to 80 percent of the volume of a testis; the interstitium makes up an estimated 20 to 30 percent of the volume.

The interstitium is an important exchange area of the testis: Here, fluid and key molecules enter and leave the blood vessels, and excess tissue fluid enters the lymphatic vessels. Exchange is not limited to liquids. Certain blood cells also have the ability to move from the circulatory system to the tissue fluid to the lymphatic system in the interstitium.

The Testicle

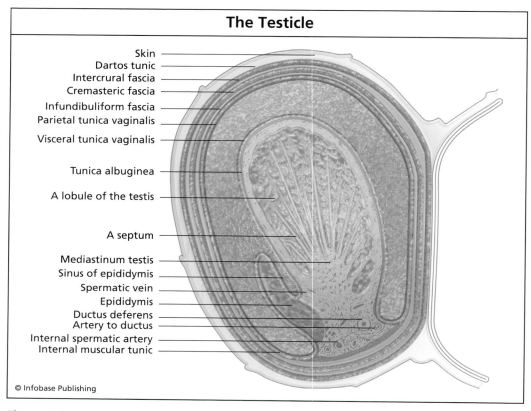

Skin
Dartos tunic
Intercrural fascia
Cremasteric fascia
Infundibuliform fascia
Parietal tunica vaginalis
Visceral tunica vaginalis

Tunica albuginea

A lobule of the testis

A septum

Mediastinum testis
Sinus of epididymis
Spermatic vein
Epididymis
Ductus deferens
Artery to ductus
Internal spermatic artery
Internal muscular tunic

© Infobase Publishing

Figure 4.1

Leydig cells of the interstitium are capable of becoming cancer cells. Because a Leydig cell is not a germ cell (i.e., it is *not* a cell that will develop into a sperm), a Leydig cell cancer is considered a non–germ cell cancer.

SPERM PRODUCTION IN THE TESTES

Each testis of a male who has gone through puberty has many hundreds (estimates range from 500 to more than 1,000) of U-shaped seminiferous tubules actively engaged in **spermatogenesis**, the process by which millions of sperm cells are produced each day. The looped tubules are also coiled; looping and coiling enables more of these important structures to fit into the confined space of the testis. If stretched out, each tubule would be about a foot or two in length; if the many hundreds of seminiferous tubules from a testis were stretched out and placed end to end, they would cover the length of at least two football fields! Sperm production occurs along the entire length of a seminiferous tubule.

Seminiferous tubules have walls that surround the open area in the center, called the lumen. Sperm made in the wall, along with fluid that enables these cells to be moved through the tubule, are released into the lumen of the tubules. The walls of the seminiferous tubules are made of cells dedicated to sperm production (the **germinal epithelium**) and underlying supportive tissue. The cells of the germinal epithelium of the seminiferous tubule walls are of two types: germ cells (cells in various stages of sperm development) and Sertoli cells (cells that aid developing germ cells). The rest of the seminiferous tubule is made of supportive tissues that surround the germinal epithelium. Immediately underlying the germinal epithelium is the basement membrane. The tissue layer is made of structural molecules, such as the protein collagen, that physically support the germinal epithelium and also connect it to the underlying loose connective tissue, the peritubular tissue (literally, tissue around the tube). This tissue, which is also composed of molecules such as collagen, plays a structural role. Cells that can produce connective tissue molecules are present in the peritubular tissue, and researchers are learning that these cells also communicate with—and influence—cells of the germinal epithelium.

These testis cells and the many other non–germ cells have a variety of functions, all of which are directed at assisting in the primary function

Figure 4.2 This color scanning electron micrograph (SEM) image shows the seminiferous tubules. The center of each seminiferous tubule is filled with developing sperm, of which the tails can be seen (blue). (© *Susumu Nishinaga/ Photo Researchers, Inc.*)

of the testes: to enable sexual reproduction through the production and release of sperm. It is sperm, and the cells from which they are derived, that are the testes' germ cells, a broad term that encompasses cells in four categories:

1. Cells in the developing embryo/fetus that are the precursors of spermatogonia (**primordial germ cells** and the **gonocytes** derived from them)

2. Cells derived from gonocytes that have the ability to divide in order to copy themselves or to produce cells that will develop into sperm cells (**spermatogonia**; sometimes referred to as spermatogenic stem cells)

3. Cells derived from spermatogonia (**primary spermatocytes, secondary spermatocytes**, and **spermatids**) that are in various stages along the developmental pathway toward becoming sperm cells

4. Spermatozoa, or sperm cells

Some of these germ cells develop into germ cell tumors. Evidence gathered by researchers indicates that cells early in the germ cell developmental pathway are the ones that become cancer cells, but this remains an active area of investigation. One of the challenges faced by scientists is that there is still much to be learned about the many changes that occur as these cells proceed along the normal development pathway: from primordial germ cell formation to mature sperm.

The process of spermatogenesis begins in puberty as spermatogonia divide (by a process known as **mitosis**) to produce two cell types: (1) cells that are copies of the original cell (which ensure that the supply of stem cells will not be depleted) and (2) cells that will develop into primary spermatocytes.

A primary spermatocyte undergoes two rounds of a special type of cell division called **meiosis**. The first division of the primary spermatocyte produces two secondary spermatocytes. Each secondary spermatocyte undergoes division to produce two cells called spermatids. Thus, each primary spermatocyte ultimately produces a total of four spermatids. The arrangement of germ cells in the germinal epithelium reflects the stages of their development: spermatogonia lie in the outer region of the germinal epithelium (farthest from the lumen and closest to the basement membrane), the spermatocytes are closer to the lumen, and the spermatids are closest to the lumen.

Meiosis is the type of cell division that produces gametes, sperm in males and eggs in females. The result of division by meiosis (rather than by mitosis) is that the spermatids have half the number of chromosomes as the primary spermatocytes, 23 instead of 46. This halving of the number of chromosomes is essential for successful sexual reproduction; if it did not occur, the amount of chromosomal DNA would double in each successive generation. The process of meiosis is precise, and the number of chromosomes is not randomly cut in half. Like all of the body, or **somatic** cells, each primary spermatocyte is **diploid**, meaning it has two copies of each chromosome, one from the mother (maternal) and the other from the father (paternal). Imagine that there are 23 pairs of chromosomes, each carrying a sign with a numeral from 1 to 23. The cell would have two chromosomes marked 1, two chromosomes labeled 2, and so on through chromosome pair 23. Meiosis ensures that each cell will get one of each chromosome 1 through 23. Meiosis reduces the chromosome number so that each spermatid is **haploid**, having only one copy of each chromosome. It is in the zygote stage, after the maternal and paternal DNA have come together, that the diploid number is restored.

Each spermatid develops into a sperm cell by a process known as **spermiogenesis**, a process of cell differentiation (i.e., a cell becoming specialized) and not cell division. A number of things occur during spermiogenesis: the cell's DNA and nucleus undergo changes, cytoplasm is removed, a flagellum that will enable the cell to move in the female reproductive tract develops, and a cap of enzymes that will be later used in fertilization is formed.

The entire process—from primary spermatocyte to mature sperm—takes about 60 days.

SERTOLI CELLS

Sertoli cells assist in many ways with the development of sperm cells. These large cells span the germinal epithelium, from the basement membrane to the lumen, and lie side by side, forming a continuous layer of cells around the tubule.

The sides of the Sertoli cells are attached tightly to each other by specialized connections, preventing fluid, dissolved molecules, and cells from moving between the Sertoli cells. As a result, molecules must pass through the cytoplasm of Sertoli cells to move from the lumen-side of Sertoli cells to the basement membrane-side of Sertoli cells. This lack of free movement of materials between cells is an important contributor to the **blood-testis barrier**, a system that restricts access to the developing sperm cells by molecules and immune cells from the blood and prevents sperm cells from gaining access to immune cells. The evolutionary advantage of the barrier is thought to be protection of the developing sperm from the body's immune system, which would recognize these cells as foreign and destroy them.

Germ cells develop in pocketlike projections of the Sertoli cells, moving closer to the lumen as they mature. This requires breaking and reforming of the connections between Sertoli cells. Sertoli cells secrete a variety of molecules, including androgen-binding protein that concentrates testosterone, and hormones; they also engulf spermatid cytoplasm and secrete the fluid that helps carry sperm through the seminiferous tubule.

Sertoli cells are capable of developing into cancer cells. Because a Sertoli cell is not a germ cell, a Sertoli cell cancer is considered a non–germ cell cancer.

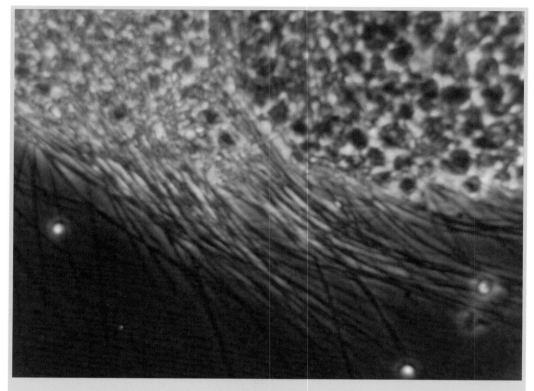

Figure 4.3   Sperm surround a Sertoli cell, which provides nourishment for developing sperm. *(© LookatSciences/Phototake)*

THE PASSAGE OF SPERM OUT OF THE BODY

Sperm produced along the length of a seminiferous tubule can leave through either end, as both converge on a meshwork of tubules called the **rete testis.** This collects sperm and fluid from all of the seminiferous tubules and is located in the mediastinum testis. Although rare, cells of the rete testis can become cancer cells, resulting in cancer of the rete testis.

Sperm leave the rete testis (and the testis itself) at the hilus by way of 6 to 12 small tubes known as **efferent ductules**. These carry the sperm to the epididymis, a collection tube that lies just outside the testis.

The highly coiled epididymis (which would be about 16 feet if stretched out) runs along the back of the testis. In the first section, much of the fluid produced in the seminiferous tubules is reabsorbed, concentrating the sperm. The rest of the epididymis serves as more than a simple conduit for sperm: It is where the sperm mature to the point at which they are able to successfully fertilize an ovum. Sperm are also stored in the epididymis until they leave the scrotal area to be released from the penis through ejaculation.

Sperm leave the epididymis by way of the vas deferens, which carries sperm from the scrotum, through the inguinal canal, and into the abdominal cavity. (In the male sterilization procedure known as a vasectomy, the vasa deferentia—one vas deferens on each side of the body—are cut.) In the abdominal cavity, the vas deferens loops up and over the bladder, the structure that stores urine. Sperm are propelled through the vas deferens by contractions of the muscles that surround the tube. Just near its end, the vas deferens is renamed the **ejaculatory duct**.

The short ejaculatory ducts on each side of the body join with the urethra—the tube that carries urine from the bladder. The urethra serves two important functions: It delivers sperm and urine (at separate times) to the outside of the body through the penis. The urethra is the first—and only—tube where sperm traveling from the right testicle and sperm traveling from the left testicle join. All the other tubes through which sperm travel are present on both sides of the body.

Figure 4.4   These sperm are moving from the seminiferous tubules through the rete testis. From there the sperm will finish developing and be stored in the epididymis. *(© Innerspace Imaging/Photo Researchers, Inc.)*

Fluid, known as **seminal fluid**, is added to the sperm in the vas deferens and the urethra by specialized glands. The combination of sperm and seminal fluid, the material released from the urethra during ejaculation, is known as **semen**.

THE CIRCULATORY SYSTEM AND THE TESTIS

The circulatory system carries blood through blood vessels (arteries, arterioles, veins, venules, and capillaries) that are distributed throughout the body. Blood consists of fluid (plasma), red and white blood cells, and platelets. Important molecules, such as nutrients and hormones, are carried in the plasma. Red blood cells carry oxygen to the body's tissues, the many types of white blood cells work in complex ways to help the body defend itself from microbes and cancer cells, and platelets assist in blood clotting. Under pressure from the pumping heart, blood is pushed through arteries and the smaller arterioles, tubes that carry blood away from the heart, eventually reaching the capillaries, the vessels of the body that exchange materials with body tissues. This exchange is possible because capillaries have thin walls, made only of a single layer of cells known as endothelial cells. Plasma (and at times white blood cells) leaves the blood by passing between endothelial cells, allowing the fluid (now referred to as tissue fluid) to bathe body tissues. Molecules can then be exchanged between the cells of the body tissues and the tissue fluid. Much of the tissue fluid is eventually returned to the circulatory system, moving back into the capillaries. From capillaries, the fluid travels in venules to larger veins back to the heart.

The blood supply for the testes comes largely from the testicular arteries. These two arteries branch from the aorta—the body's main artery that carries blood from the heart—as it runs through the retroperitoneal cavity. They are then routed through the spermatic cord; the right testicular artery delivers blood to the right testis and the left testicular artery delivers blood to the left testis. Once at the testis, the artery branches, supplying all areas of the testis. Many of the branches travel along connective tissue to the individual lobules. Capillaries in the interstitium exchange with the local tissue fluid. Although some of these capillaries are near the seminiferous tubules, the seminiferous tubules do not have their own capillary supply: Exchange occurs with the capillaries of the interstitium.

Fluid and molecules reenter the capillaries and move to venules, then to larger veins. The veins that leave the testis join other veins to form a network of veins in the spermatic cord known as the **pampiniform plexus**. From the plexus, two testicular veins enter the retroperitoneum where they return blood to the inferior vena cava—the main vessel that returns blood to the heart from the lower part of the body—or to a branch of the inferior vena cava.

THE LYMPHATIC SYSTEM AND THE TESTIS

Although most tissue fluid eventually returns to the circulatory system through capillaries, about 1 percent does not. This excess fluid enters another system of the body: the lymphatic system. Like the circulatory system, the lymphatic system has vessels through which fluid moves. But unlike the circulatory system, these vessels do not form a continuous loop. Rather, lymph capillaries of this one-way system pick up fluid (which at this point is referred to as **lymph**) from tissues. They then join progressively larger vessels (lymph veins) and ultimately a large vessel—a duct—through which the fluid is returned to the circulatory system. In the lymphatic system, there is no heart that pumps, there are no arteries or arterioles, and capillaries only *collect* fluid from the tissues.

The lymphatic system does much more, however, than return fluid to the circulatory system: It is intimately involved with the body's immune system, which defends the body against infectious microbes and cancer cells. The lymphatic system contributes to this defense in two important ways:

1. Cells (microbes and cancer cells) as well as tissue fluid can be picked up by lymph capillaries.

2. As this material moves through lymph vessels on its way to the circulatory system, it encounters lymph nodes, small structures that filter lymph. Lymph vessels empty lymph into one end of a lymph node. The lymph moves slowly through the meshlike node, eventually leaving through a lymph vessel on the opposite side. The lymph node is more than a mechanical filter. Cells in a lymph node trap, destroy, and become activated to destroy microbes and cancer cells. (Some cancer cells trapped by lymph nodes survive and multiply within the node, but without the lymph nodes, these cancer cells would enter the bloodstream unchecked.)

In the testis, many lymph capillaries, like the blood capillaries, are located in the interstitium. They join others, leaving the testis as larger lymphatic vessels at the hilus. They enter the spermatic cord, then travel to the retroperitoneal cavity. From there, vessels join a long and much larger vessel, the thoracic duct, which returns lymph to the left subclavian vein, located near the heart. Testicular cancer cells that are picked up by lymphatic capillaries in the testes first encounter lymph nodes in the retroperitoneal cavity. These retroperitoneal lymph nodes are therefore usually the first landing sites for testicular cancer metastases.

SUMMARY

The testes are formed during fetal life in the retroperitoneum, a space at the back of abdominal cavity. As development proceeds, they move through the inguinal canals into the scrotum. Each remains connected to the abdomen through its spermatic cord. The spermatic cord contains blood vessels, lymph vessels, and a tube that carries sperm from the testes. Sperm are made in the testes in long tubes known as seminifer-ous tubules. Production of sperm takes many weeks, and is a stepwise process that involves cell division and cell changes. Sertoli cells, located in seminiferous tubules, help in the process of sperm development. Leydig cells, located in tissue between seminiferous tubules, produce the hormone testosterone.

5

GERM CELL CANCERS

KEY POINTS

- Most testicular cancers are germ cell cancers.

- Germ cell cancers are categorized as either seminomatous or non-seminomatous.

- Seminomatous germ cell cancers include seminoma and spermato-cytic seminoma, a cancer that occurs in older men.

- Nonseminomatous germ cell cancers include embryonal carcinoma, yolk sac tumor, trophoblastic tumors (primarily choriocarcinoma), and teratoma.

- Germ cell tumors that are mixtures of more than one tumor type are called mixed germ cell tumors. They are classified with the non-seminomatous germ cell cancers because of the way they respond to available treatments.

MOST TESTICULAR CANCERS ARE GERM CELL CANCERS

Baseball player Mike Lowell, cyclist Lance Armstrong, skater Scott Hamilton, newscaster Sean Kimerling, and high school student Jason Struble share a diagnosis of testicular cancer: They also have in common the *type* of testicular cancer with which they were diagnosed: a germ cell cancer.

There are many different types of testicular cancer. Of these, several develop from germ cells—cells in sperm's developmental pathway—and are therefore classified as germ cell cancers. Most testicular cancers are germ cell cancers; in males who have gone through puberty, more than 90 percent of testicular cancers fall into this category.

There are many different types of germ cell cancer. The type of germ cell tumor (GCT) a patient has is determined in the laboratory. The pathologist determines the way the tumor looks to the eye as well as histologically, when stained slices are examined under a microscope. Immunohistochemistry can add important diagnostic clues by showing whether certain cell-specific molecules are present. Serum tumor marker information can also assist in tumor identification.

Germ cell tumor classification has changed over time, and there is variation in how GCTs are classified from one part of the world to another. The United States and many other countries use the classification scheme of the World Health Organization (WHO). In the WHO system, GCTs are classified as either pure (composed of one histological—or tissue—type) or mixed (composed of more than one histological type). The pure histological types of GCTs are seminoma, **spermatocytic seminoma**, **embryonal carcinoma**, yolk sac tumor, **trophoblastic tumors**, and **teratoma**. Mixed GCTs are made up of varying combinations of these types.

For testicular cancers other than seminoma and spermatocytic seminoma, the transformed cell types become very different from germ cells. They change to take on some properties that are similar to cells of early embryos (as in embryonal carcinoma); more developed embryos, fetuses, and adults (as in teratoma); or **extraembryonic membranes,** structures that are attached to an embryo and assist in its development (as in yolk sac tumor and trophoblastic tumors).

◆ EARLY HUMAN DEVELOPMENT

After a few days of cell division, the mammalian zygote develops into a blastocyst (a hollow structure with an inner cell mass that will become the fetus) and a chorion made of trophoblasts, which will form the fetal part of the placenta.

As the blastocyst implants into the lining of the uterus, the chorion develops to form two placenta-producing layers (the cytotrophoblast and the synctiotrophoblast). The inner cell mass forms two layers: the endoderm and the ectoderm. Later, a third layer, the mesoderm, will form. Trophoblasts, cytotrophoblasts, and synctiotrophoblasts secrete hCG.

Later in embryonic development, a well-developed yolk sac appears. The yolk sac is the structure that is responsible for production of a fetus's first blood cells and primordial germ cells. The placenta, the structure that connects and exchanges materials between the fetus and the mother, is also well developed.

The yolk sac and chorion are both extraembryonic membranes, structures that are attached to a developing embryo and assist in its development.

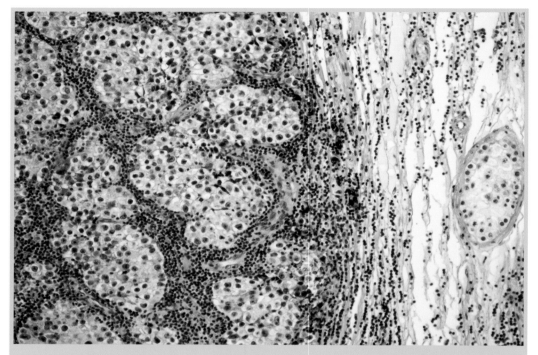

Figure 5.1 This light micrograph shows a section of a seminoma, a type of germ cell cancer (lower left). *(© CNRI/Photo Researchers, Inc.)*

Physicians and researchers group these different tumor types into two categories: seminomatous GCTs (seminomas) and nonseminomatous GCTs (nonseminomas). This categorization, while artificial, is useful because it reflects not only the differences noted (the presence or absence of properties shared with developing embryos/fetuses/adults), but also differences in how tumors can be treated by doctors. Seminomas respond to radiation and chemotherapy, while nonseminomas respond only to chemotherapy and often require more aggressive treatment.

Nonseminomatous GCTs include embryonal carcinoma, yolk sac tumor, trophoblastic tumors, teratoma, and mixed GCTs. Seminomatous

GCTs include seminoma (sometimes referred to as classic seminoma) and the less common and quite different spermatocytic seminoma. Because spermatocytic seminoma is so different, often the term seminomatous GCT is used to refer only to seminoma.

Some mixed GCTs have seminoma as a component. Why, then, are all mixed GCTs—regardless of the presence of seminoma—classified as nonseminomas? The reason is related to treatment: If the tumor is treated as a nonseminoma, both the seminoma and the nonseminomatous component will respond; if the tumor is treated as a seminoma, only the seminoma component will respond.

GERM CELL TUMORS IN BOYS AND OLDER MEN

Most individuals who develop testicular cancer do so between the onset of puberty and their mid-forties. But testicular cancer can also occur in boys (males before puberty) and older men. For all age groups, the most common type of tumor is a GCT, although these represent a smaller fraction—only about two-thirds—of the testicular tumors in boys.

The distribution of GCT types differs among age groups. Spermatocytic seminoma occurs mostly in men older than 50, and it never occurs in men younger than 30. In adults, the most common GCTs are seminoma (about 50 percent of the cases), mixed GCT (a little less than 50 percent), and embryonal carcinoma (less than 10 percent). In boys, yolk sac tumor and teratoma are the most common GCT types, while seminoma and embryonal carcinoma occur only rarely.

The differences are not just in tumor incidence. Scientists have discovered that there are genetic differences between GCT cells that occur in boys, those that occur in men, and spermatocytic seminoma.

♦ EXTRAGONADAL GERM CELL TUMORS

Testicular germ cell tumors can metastasize to parts of the body far from the testicle, such as the retroperitoneum and the mediastinum, an area of the chest. But sometimes, a testicular GCT can occur in these areas in the apparent absence of a testicular GCT. These are known as **extragonadal germ cell tumors** (EGGCTs). The term extragonadal implies that these primary tumors (tumors that have developed in—rather than metastasized to—a location) occur *outside* the gonad. Another common location for EGGCTs is a gland in the brain known as the pineal gland.

At times, a physician may discover that the mass is not a true EGGCT because a small mass can actually be found in the testicle. But many appear to be true EGGCTs.

A commonly accepted explanation for the presence of these tumors is that an error occurred during migration of primordial germ cells in the fetus; instead of migrating from the yolk sac to the primitive testis developing in the abdomen, the germ cells traveled to a different area, such as the mediastinum. But researchers are exploring other hypotheses. One is that cells in a testis that have started to, but not yet, become cancer cells migrate from the testes to other areas; only when they reach these other areas do they become cancer cells.

Brian Piccolo, football player for the Chicago Bears, died in 1969 at the age of 26 of embryonal carcinoma that originated in the mediastinum. Thankfully, advancements in the treatment of this type of cancer have been made since the 1960s. His story was told in the film *Brian's Song*.

It appears that GCTs in these three categories have different causes and pathways of development.

There are also interesting differences between teratomas that occur before and after puberty. Teratoma in children is always benign—it does not invade neighboring tissues or spread to other parts of the body by metastasis. In adults, teratoma can be benign but it can also be malignant, spreading to nearby tissues and capable of spreading to distant sites. An additional age-related difference is that teratoma in children is almost always a pure tumor, while in adults it is usually found as a component of a mixed GCT. The reasons for these differences are not understood.

SEMINOMA

Seminoma (classic seminoma) is the most common type of GCT found in adults. About half of the GCTs in adults are seminomas, and seminoma is a component of many mixed GCTs. Seminoma is rarely found in boys, and occurs mostly in men in their mid-thirties to mid-forties. This is later in life than adult nonseminomas tend to occur.

The main symptom for most seminoma patients is an enlarged but pain-free testicle. A small percentage of seminoma patients may also have enlarged breast tissue (gynecomastia). If the tumor has metastasized, symptoms may be felt in parts of the body to which the cancer has spread, most commonly the abdomen. For most patients, however, the tumor has not metastasized at the time of diagnosis.

Sometimes the tumor will spread locally to nearby structures such as the epididymis or spermatic cord. Seminoma spreads to distant areas through the lymphatic system: first to retroperitoneal lymph nodes, and later to lymph nodes in the middle of the chest (mediastinal) and above the collarbone. The disease can spread further still by way of the circulatory system, to sites such as the liver, lung, and bones.

In some cases, seminoma cells secrete hCG, which is detectable in low concentration in the blood. hCG can cause gynecomastia. Seminoma cells never secrete AFP, which is an important factor in certain diagnoses. For example, if the histology shows pure seminoma but blood tests show elevated concentrations of AFP, a doctor will know that the tumor is not seminoma, but actually a mixed GCT (nonseminoma) that will require different treatment.

When a pathologist cuts into a seminoma tumor, it appears light in color. There is no significant necrosis (dead tissue) or hemorrhage (bleeding). The tumor is homogeneous, meaning that different areas of the tumor are similar in appearance.

After staining the sample with hematoxylin-eosin, microscopic examination shows that the cells are organized to form sheets of neatly arranged cells, commonly in clusters that are separated by connective tissue in which many white blood cells, especially lymphocytes, have gathered. Neighboring cells do not overlap. The cells are fairly uniform in appearance, and cell features such as a cell membrane, cytoplasm, and nucleus with one or more nucleoli are easily seen.

A challenge for pathologists is the existence of forms of seminoma that vary in cell characteristics and cell arrangement and differ from the normal microscopic appearance. Some variants may look like other tumor types. In one variant, syncytiotrophoblasts, large cells with many nuclei per cell, are found among the typical cells.

SPERMATOCYTIC SEMINOMAS

Spermatocytic seminoma is not a variant of seminoma; it is a unique type of GCT. It accounts for only a small percentage of testicular cancers. Most commonly, the disease occurs in men older than 50. It occasionally occurs in younger men, but not in those under 30. Unlike other histological types, spermatocytic seminoma is never a component of GCTs.

The primary symptom is a painless mass in the testis. The tumor may invade local tissues such as the epididymis, but it rarely metastasizes. A patient's prognosis is therefore excellent. The cut surface of the tumor is light in color, and some tumors may have small areas of necrosis or hemorrhage.

Microscopically, one characteristic of spermatocytic seminoma is the presence of three cell types that differ in size: small, intermediate (the predominant cell type), and large. These cells are not arranged in well-organized sheets as in seminoma. Groups of cells are often separated by areas that have only a small amount of connective tissue and may be filled with fluid.

Even though prognosis is usually excellent, on occasion, parts of the tumor change to form a sarcoma, a connective-tissue-like tumor. The sarcoma may metastasize to the retroperitoneum and organs. Currently, prognosis for these patients is poor.

EMBRYONAL CARCINOMA

Embryonal carcinoma is the most common nonseminomatous, pure GCT in adults, but it is much less common than seminoma and mixed GCTs, accounting for less than 10 percent of adult GCTs. It tends to occur in men between their mid-twenties and mid-thirties, about 10 years earlier than seminoma. It rarely occurs before puberty and is a component of more than 80 percent of mixed GCTs.

Embryonal carcinoma is usually noticed because of a mass in the testis. Often, but not always, the mass is painless. Gynecomastia may occur. Many patients have metastases at the time of diagnosis and may have symptoms resulting from the spread to lymph nodes or organs.

Sometimes the cancer invades local structures such as the epididymis and spermatic cord. It metastasizes via the lymphatics to the retroperitoneal and mediastinal lymph nodes. At times, it may spread through the blood, often to the lungs. Some tumors make hCG, which can be detected in the blood serum.

When a tumor of this type is examined in the lab, large areas of necrosis and hemorrhage are typically seen. Microscopically, the cells are large and have different shapes and they tend to overlap. Many cells appear to be in the process of division, and abnormalities in the division process can be seen. Syncytiotrophoblasts may be present.

Embryonal carcinoma cells are undifferentiated—they are not mature cells with a set function. Many of the cells look like epithelial cells, which cover surfaces of the body; in some areas, they are even arranged like epithelial cells around cavities, forming structures that look roughly like glands. Embryonal carcinoma cells can be arranged in many different patterns, and a pathologist must be able to recognize them all.

YOLK SAC TUMOR

Yolk sac tumor is the most common testicular cancer in children. The name comes from the fact that the tumor has characteristics—such as AFP production—that are similar to the embryonic yolk sac. It occurs in boys from infancy to age 11; the median age is about 16 months. Yolk sac tumor also appears in adults, but almost always as a component of mixed GCTs. About 40 percent of mixed GCTs contain yolk sac tumor.

◆ IMMUNOHISTOCHEMISTRY AND TESTICULAR CANCER TYPES

Immunohistochemistry can be used to distinguish one testicular cancer type from another. For example, what if the pathologist wants to determine if a tumor is seminoma or embryonal carcinoma? Cells of these two cancers have many molecules in common, including a surface protein known as placental alkaline phosphatase (PLAP). Detection of such molecules *cannot* help tell the two cancer types apart. However, the cells of the two cancers differ in the presence of other surface molecules, such as c-Kit, Ki-1, and podopladin. The difference in the presence of these proteins can help tell the two cancers apart: Seminoma cells, but not those of embryonal carcinoma, have c-Kit and podopladin on the surface; embryonal carcinoma cells, but not those of seminoma, have Ki-1.

Scientists continue to look for cellular molecules that can identify particular cancer cells. They are also interested in gaining a better understanding of the normal roles of these proteins, as well as their relationship to the development of particular cancers.

PLAP is an enzyme that is normally made by trophoblasts of the chorion. The normal function of podopladin is unclear, but it has been found in fetal germ cells, and has been suggested to play a role in fetal germ cell development. Ki-1 and c-Kit are receptor molecules; each allows the cell to detect and respond to a particular outside chemical signal. These are normally made by certain blood cells.

Yolk sac tumors are usually discovered by parents who notice that a child's testicle has rapidly enlarged. In about 10 to 20 percent of children, the tumor has metastasized at time of diagnosis. Metastasis may occur via the lymphatics to the retroperitoneal lymph nodes. Often, however, spread is through the blood only; for these patients, the first site of metastasis is often the lungs.

Almost all yolk sac tumors, including mixed GCTs that contain yolk sac tumor cells, make AFP, and detection of elevated serum AFP can help to identify yolk sac tumor as a component of a mixed GCT. When the tumors are large, necrosis and hemorrhage are often present.

Two tumor features that can be seen microscopically are crucial to diagnosis: the presence of multiple histological patterns (characteristic cell arrangements) in a single tumor, and the presence of structures known as Schiller-Duval bodies, collections of cancer cells that surround fingerlike, blood-vessel containing projections of connective tissue. Commonly, hyaline globules, collections of AFP (or another protein) normally produced by the yolk sac, are also present.

CHORIOCARCINOMA

Almost all trophoblastic tumors fall into the category of **choriocarcinoma**. The name comes from its similarity to the chorion, which forms the fetal part of the placenta.

Choriocarcinoma occurs only very rarely (less than 1 percent of cases) in pure form. Most men diagnosed with this form of cancer are in their teens and twenties. Choriocarcinoma occurs in about 8 percent of mixed GCTs. Choriocarcinoma spreads rapidly and widely, and has the worst prognosis of all the germ cell cancers.

Choriocarcinoma differs from other germ cell cancers in presentation: Most patients seek medical help from the symptoms of metastasis and not the tumor itself. Often, by the time of diagnosis, the tumor has regressed (shrunk).

Choriocarcinoma spreads through the blood to the lungs and often to the liver, gastrointestinal tract, brain, and other organs. It also spreads through the lymphatic system to the retroperitoneal lymph nodes. Symptoms include shortness of breath, coughing up or vomiting blood, and dark stools (due to gastrointestinal bleeding). Bleeding can occur in many areas of the body, causing anemia (too few red blood cells). Neurological problems that result from spread to the brain can also occur. The high concentrations of hCG may cause gynecomastia and an underactive thyroid (a gland that controls metabolism).

Microscopically, choriocarcinoma has two main cell types: syncytiotrophoblasts and cytotrophoblasts. These cells are arranged in varying patterns. The two cell types normally compose the placenta-forming extraembryonic membrane known as the chorion. Like trophoblast cells of the chorion, these cells produce large quantities of hCG. While hCG is sometimes produced in other types of testicular cancer, it is always secreted in large concentrations in choriocarcinoma.

TERATOMA

The word teratoma comes from the Greek word for monster (*teraton*) and reflects the fact that the tumor is an odd conglomeration of recognizable tissues. Although not in testicular cancer, other types of teratomas can actually have hair and teeth.

Pure teratoma rarely occurs in adults; only about 2 to 3 percent of adult GCTs are teratomas. Teratoma occurs frequently as part of mixed GCTs in adults; about half of these tumors contain teratoma. Pure teratoma occurs more commonly in children. Some feel that the pediatric percentage is underreported because teratoma is benign in this population. Most teratomas in children occur in those younger than four years of age, and most often in one- and two-year-olds.

There are two types of teratoma: mature and immature. A mature teratoma has adultlike, differentiated cells only. Usually several types of tissue are present in one tumor. For example, tumors might have neural tissue, bone, and cartilage. An immature teratoma may also have adult-like differentiated cells, but less differentiated cells (more embryonic, or fetal-like) are also present. These less-differentiated cells, however, are *more* differentiated than those seen in embryonal carcinoma. Some teratomas have tissues from only a single germ layer (monodermal teratoma), while others have tissues from two, or all three, germ layers. What is a germ layer? As normal embryonic development proceeds, cells of the inner cell mass begin to differentiate, taking on specific structures and roles. As part of this process, three layers of tissue (germ layers) form in the embryo: the ectoderm, the endoderm, and the mesoderm. The ectoderm is on the outside and will eventually develop into adult structures such as the epidermis (outer skin layer) and nervous system. The endoderm is on the inside and will develop into adult tissues that line body cavities such as the lungs and digestive tract. The mesoderm, in the middle, will develop into tissues such as muscle and bone.

The difference between pre- and postpuberty teratomas is that most teratomas that occur before puberty are mature, while most that occur after puberty are immature. Both immature and mature adult teratomas can metastasize.

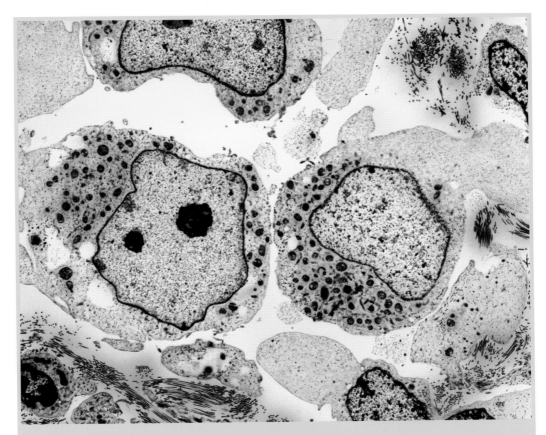

Figure 5.2 A color transmission electron micrograph (TEM) shows three malignant teratoma cells. Each teratoma cell shown here has a large, irregular-shaped nucleus (brown). *(© Steve Gschmeissner/Photo Researchers, Inc.)*

In children, because there is never metastasis, the only symptom is a testicular mass. Adults may present with a mass or symptoms of metastasis.

The pathologist will note that the cut tumor surface is not homogenous—different tissue types can be seen in different areas of the tumor. Cysts filled with fluid of different consistencies are commonly found.

Microscopically, cells, some of which appear abnormal compared to their normal counterparts, are arranged to form tissues. At times, these different tissues can be seen arranged to form primitive organlike structures, such as skin. Synctiotrophoblasts may be present.

MIXED GERM CELL TUMORS

Mixed GCTs normally occur only in males who have gone through puberty. Any of the different GCT types, with the exception of spermatocytic seminoma, may be present in a single tumor. After seminoma, mixed GCTs are the most common type of adult GCT.

More than 80 percent of mixed GCTs have embryonal carcinoma as one of the components, and about half contain teratoma. Yolk sac tumor and seminoma occur less frequently, but are still commonly found. Choriocarcinoma is found in less than 10 percent of the mixed GCTs.

The different tumor types vary in aggressiveness, metastasis locations, and treatment sensitivity, and so it is important for the pathologist to list the different tumor types and to estimate the percentage of each. This information will affect treatment decisions.

SUMMARY

GCTs arise from germ cells and are the most common type of testicular cancer. The type of GCT a patient has is determined by analysis of the tumor in the pathology lab and by the presence or absence of certain tumor markers in the blood. It is important to diagnose the type of GCT accurately because they may require different treatment. GCTs are grouped into two large categories: seminomatous GCTs and nonseminomatous GCTs. Seminomatous GCTs are of two types: seminoma (classic seminoma) and spermatocytic seminoma, which occurs in older men. Nonseminomatous GCTs include embryonal carcinoma, yolk sac tumor, trophoblastic tumors (primarily choriocarcinoma), and teratoma. Some GCTs are made of more than one tumor type and are known as mixed GCTs. These tumors (some of which may contain seminoma) are classified as nonseminomatous for treatment purposes. The most commonly diagnosed GCTs in young men are seminoma and mixed GCT. In boys, yolk sac tumor and teratoma are prevalent.

6

NON-GERM CELL TESTICULAR TUMORS

KEY POINTS

- Non-germ cell testicular tumors are much less common than germ cell tumors.

- Non-germ cell tumors make up a greater percentage of the testicular tumors that occur in boys than those that occur in adults.

- Leydig cell tumors, Sertoli cell tumors, rete testis carcinoma, and primary testicular lymphoma are non-germ cell tumors of the testis.

- Some non-germ cell tumors are benign. Many of the malignant forms carry a poor prognosis.

Testicular tumors that arise from cells that support germ cells or play other roles in testicular function—non-germ cell testicular tumors—occur much less frequently than their germ cell tumor counterparts. Testicular tumors that do not arise from germ cells represent a greater proportion of testicular tumors in children than in adults. Some of these tumors are benign, but others are malignant. Unfortunately, the great success in the treatment of germ cell tumors has not been replicated for non-germ cell tumors, and many still carry a poor prognosis. There are many different types of non-germ cell tumors; in this chapter, Leydig cell tumors, Sertoli cell tumors, carcinoma of the rete testis, and testicular lymphoma are described.

LEYDIG CELL TUMORS

Leydig cell tumors (LCTs) account for about 1 to 3 percent of testicular tumors. About 25 percent of LCTs occur in children, generally between the ages of 5 and 10, and are benign. About 10 percent of adult LCTs are malignant. Malignant LCTs respond poorly to existing treatments, so prognosis is poor. LCTs produce sex hormones (predominately testosterone, and at times estrogen), which in many cases cause body changes. These changes may appear when the tumor is small, before it can be felt in the testis. If a testosterone-producing tumor occurs in someone who has not yet gone through puberty, it will most likely cause precocious, or early, puberty. The hormonal effects of such a tumor are usually not noticed postpuberty because of background testosterone. If an estrogen-producing tumor occurs before puberty, symptoms such as gynecomastia and poor development of the gonads and genitals may occur. Postpuberty, symptoms include gynecomastia, decreased libido, and erectile dysfunction. Even after tumor removal, these effects from estrogen may persist.

SERTOLI CELL TUMORS

Sertoli cell tumors (SCTs) occur less frequently than LCTs: They account for less than 1 percent of testicular tumors. The most common type is

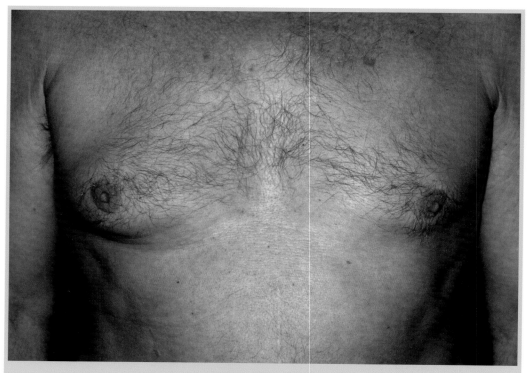

Figure 6.1   Gynecomastia, or enlargement of male breast tissue (left), is caused by an elevated level of the hormone estrogen. Some testicular tumors produce excess amounts of this hormone. *(© Dr P. Marazzi/Photo Researchers, Inc.)*

SCT NOS (not otherwise specified); variants include the very rare large cell calcifying SCT (LCCSCT). As the name suggests, LCCSCTs are large and contain calcium deposits. SCT NOS typically occurs in adults, while LCCSCT is often found in younger patients. In some cases, LCCSCT occurs as part of a syndrome, such as Peutz-Jeghers, a rare genetic disorder in which patients develop intestinal polyps and have a greatly increased risk of developing various cancers. SCT NOS is rarely malignant, but some LCCSCTs are malignant. The prognosis for maligant LCCSCTs is poor.

RETE TESTIS CARCINOMA

Rete testis carcinoma is a rare tumor that arises in the sperm-collecting ducts of the testis. These tumors most commonly occur in elderly men, but are not restricted to this age group. Prognosis is poor.

LYMPHOMA

Lymphoma, a solid cancer of lymphocytes (a category of white blood cells that play key roles in the body's defense) can occur at many body sites. When the initial site is the testis, the lymphoma is referred to as primary testicular lymphoma. In adults, the most common form that occurs in the testis involves a type of lymphocyte known as a B cell—a cell that normally matures to secrete defensive proteins known as antibodies. Most primary testicular lymphomas are unilateral, meaning that one testicle is affected, but some are bilateral, meaning that both testes are affected. Primary testicular lymphoma accounts for 3 to 5 percent of testicular tumors; as with GCTs, however, the incidence of this disease appears to be increasing and it is not known why. Testicular lymphoma is the most common type of testicular cancer in older men. Prognosis is usually poor.

SUMMARY

Cells of the testis that are not germ cells, but rather support germ cells or have other functions in the testis, can also form tumors. These are referred to as non-germ cell tumors. They are much less common than GCTs, but they make up a greater proportion of testicular tumors in children than in adults. Some of these tumors are benign, but others are malignant. Non-germ cell cancers have not shared the treatment success

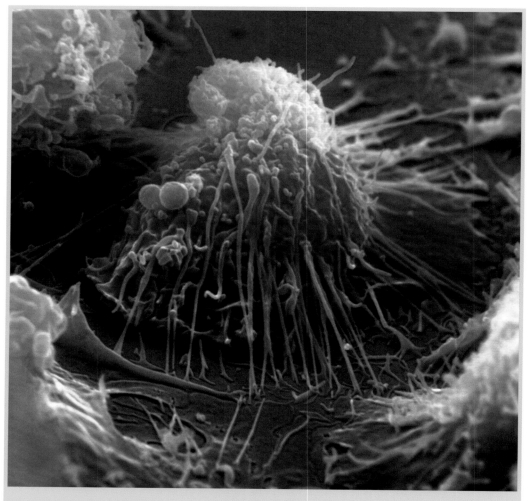

Figure 6.2   This color scanning electron micrograph (SEM) shows a normal B-lymphocyte, or B-cell. Lymphomas, or cancers of the lymphocytes, can occur in the testes and are known as primary testicular lymphomas. *(© Eye of Science/ Photo Researchers, Inc.)*

of germ cell cancers, and prognosis is often poor. Non-germ cell tumors include Leydig tumors, Sertoli cell tumors, carcinoma of the rete testis, and primary testicular lymphoma.

7

TREATMENT OF TESTICULAR CANCER

KEY POINTS

- Treatment of testicular cancer begins with an orchiectomy.

- Additional treatments, if any, depend on the type of cancer and the cancer stage.

- Testicular cancer may be in stage I (least advanced, localized), II (cancer has spread to regional lymph nodes), or III (most advanced, cancer has spread beyond regional lymph nodes).

- Additional treatments may include removal of retroperitoneal lymph nodes, chemotherapy, and radiation therapy.

- Sometimes there are no additional treatments and the patient is instead carefully monitored for signs of relapse.

Doctors performed two types of surgery to treat Scott Hamilton's testicular cancer, an orchiectomy to remove the testicle and surgery to remove retroperitoneal lymph nodes. He also underwent chemotherapy. Lance Armstrong's treatment involved an orchiectomy, chemotherapy, and surgery to remove cancer tissue from his brain. Mike Lowell's treatment involved an orchiectomy and radiation therapy. The treatments of all of these individuals began with an orchiectomy. Why was there such variation in the treatments that followed?

The initial step in the treatment (and diagnosis) of testicular cancer is the orchiectomy. Once this has been done, the decision about which additional procedures to use for a given patient is based on the type of cancer the patient has and the **cancer stage**—the extent to which the cancer has advanced and the locations to which it has spread. There is some variation among physicians in treatment preferences; variation also arises as a result of patient decisions about their treatment options.

Mike Lowell's follow-up treatment was radiation therapy alone because his cancer was a seminoma, which is sensitive to radiation. Because his disease was not advanced at the time of diagnosis, he did not need additional surgery or chemotherapy. Follow-up treatment for Scott Hamilton and Lance Armstrong did not involve radiation because they were diagnosed with nonseminoma, which is not sensitive to radiation. Because of the extent to which their cancers had spread, both chemotherapy and surgery were needed. Variation in the body locations to which their cancers had spread (the result of differences in the composition of their tumors) meant different follow-up surgeries. Hamilton's spread was typical of most nonseminomas in that it went to his retroperitoneal lymph nodes. Because Armstrong's nonseminoma was primarily choriocarcinoma, its course was different than most testicular cancers. Hence, he did not need retroperitoneal lymph node removal, but he did require surgery to remove cancer that had spread to his brain.

TESTICULAR CANCER STAGES

For testicular cancer, the cancer stages range from stage I (least advanced) to stage III (most advanced). Each of the three stages is broken down further into subcategories (i.e., IIIA, IIIB, IIIC) that further describe the details of the cancer's spread. The process of determining the cancer stage is referred to as cancer staging. In cancer staging, information about **serum** (blood fluid) tumor marker concentration is gathered, as well as information about whether the tumor has spread to tissues near the testis, to the regional lymph nodes, or to more distant sites. The staging system used to determine the extent of cancer spread is known as the **TNM (tumor-node-metastasis) system**. In this system, T stands for the spread of the tumor to nearby structures, such as the tunica vaginalis and the spermatic cord; N stands for metastasis to regional (usually retroperitoneal) lymph nodes; and M stands for metastasis of the cancer to nonregional (distant) lymph nodes or organs, such as the lungs and brain. Information about the serum (S) tumor markers AFP, hCG, and lactate dehydrogenase supplements data from the TNM system.

Cancer staging requires blood work to determine tumor marker concentration; analysis in the pathology lab of the testicle and structures near it (e.g. spermatic cord) to determine the extent of local spread; and imaging studies—such as a CT scan of the abdomen and pelvis and a chest X-ray—to look for metastasis. In addition to using the CT scan to determine whether there is metastasis to retroperitoneal lymph nodes, the determination is at times based on analysis in the pathology lab of surgically removed lymph nodes.

Table 7.1 shows the categories into which a patient's testicular cancer can be placed based on evaluation of serum tumor marker concentration (S) and information about the local spread of the primary tumor (T), its metastasis to regional lymph nodes as determined by imaging studies (N) or analysis in the pathology of excised lymph nodes (pN), and its metastasis to nonregional lymph nodes and organs (M) in the TNM system.

Table 7.2 shows testicular cancer stages based on grouping of S and TNM information. In stage I, the cancer is restricted to the testis or surrounding tissues. In stage II, the cancer has spread to the regional (usually retroperitoneal) lymph nodes, but no further. In stage III, the cancer has spread beyond the regional lymph nodes or tumor marker information suggests that it might have. When the cancer stage is determined by information gained by tissue analysis in the pathology lab, the term **pathologic stage** is used. Otherwise, the term **clinical stage** is used. The pathologic stage is more accurate.

RETROPERITONEAL LYMPH NODE DISSECTION

Testicular cancers spread in a predictable manner. In most cases, the first site of metastasis is the lymph nodes in the retroperitoneum. This predictability is good news for testicular cancer treatment, because it means that if the cancer has spread only as far as the retroperitoneum, orchiectomy followed by surgery to remove the retroperitoneal lymph nodes—a **retroperitoneal lymph node dissection (RPLND)**—can often cure the disease.

Lymph nodes in the retroperitoneum are grouped according to location within the retroperitoneum. The surgeon decides which groups of retroperitoneal lymph nodes to remove and all of the lymph nodes in those groups are removed, even if some of the individual lymph nodes do not appear to be affected.

RPLND is a treatment option for patients in clinical stage I (imaging studies show no spread to the retroperitoneum) or clinical stage II (imaging studies show spread to the retroperitoneum) who have non-seminomatous germ cell tumors (NSGCTs). In some cases, RPLND is the only treatment used. In other cases, RPLND is used in combination with chemotherapy. For advanced stages of testicular cancer, RPLND may be used to remove tissue that remains in the retroperitoneum following chemotherapy and/or radiation therapy.

Why perform a RPLND on clinical stage I patients when there is no evidence of spread to the retroperitoneum? The answer lies in the limitations of the CT scan used to determine spread to the retroperitoneal lymph nodes. Clinical stage I does not mean that the cancer has not spread to the retroperitoneum; rather, it means that imaging studies do not *show* that it has spread to the retroperitoneum. Physicians have found that it is not uncommon for the pathology lab to find metastasis to one or more nodes of clinical stage I patients. These patients were understaged by the CT scan; they were actually in pathologic stage II and not clinical stage I. For these patients, RPLND provides treatment as well as more accurate staging. Staging errors can occur in the opposite direction as well. Some patients who are placed in clinical stage II based on the CT scan are found to have no metastasis to the retroperitoneal lymph nodes on laboratory examination of the nodes.

THE DEVELOPMENT OF RPLND SURGICAL PROCEDURES

RPLND to treat testicular cancer was first performed in the early 1900s. As more physicians began to use the technique and scientists learned more about which lymph nodes could become involved by metastasis, the procedure evolved to increase the number of lymph nodes removed. By the late 1970s, the procedure involved removing lymph nodes from both sides of the retroperitoneum (bilateral RPLND), including those

TABLE 7.1	SERUM TUMOR MARKER (S) AND TNM STAGING FOR TESTICULAR CANCER.[1,2,3]
Primary Tumor (T)*	
pTx	Primary tumor cannot be assessed (orchiectomy not performed)
pT0	No evidence of primary tumor (e.g., only scar tissue is found in testis)
pT1	Tumor has not spread beyond the testicle and the epididymis. The tumor may have invaded the tunica albuginea.
pT2	Tumor has not spread beyond the testis and epididymis but has invaded blood vessels or lymphatic vessels, or the tumor has grown through the tunica albuginea and invaded the tunica vaginalis.
pT3	Tumor has invaded the spermatic cord. Blood vessels/lymphatic vessels may or may not be invaded
pT4	Tumor has invaded the scrotum. Blood vessels/lymphatic vessels may or may not be invaded
Regional Lymph Nodes Evaluated by Imaging Studies (N)	
Nx	Regional lymph nodes cannot be assessed.
N0	No metastasis to regional lymph nodes
N1	Metastasis to a lymph node that is ≤ 2 cm in greatest dimension, or metastasis to multiple lymph nodes ≤ 2 cm in greatest dimension
N2	Metastasis to one lymph node that is >2 cm ≤ 5 cm in greatest dimension, or metastasis to more than one lymph node, any one of them >2 cm but ≤ 5 cm in greatest dimension
N3	Metastasis to at least one lymph node that is > 5 cm in greatest dimension
Regional Lymph Nodes Evaluated After Removal and Analysis (pN)**	
pNx	Regional lymph nodes cannot be assessed.
pN0	No metastasis to regional lymph nodes
pN1	Metastasis with a lymph node ≤ 2 cm in greatest dimension and/or metastasis to ≤ 5 lymph nodes with none > 2 cm in greatest dimension

pN2	Metastasis with a lymph node > 2 cm but ≤ 5 cm in greatest dimension, or metastasis to > 5 lymph nodes, none > 5 cm or tumor growth outside the lymph node
pN3	Metastasis to at least one lymph node that is > 5 cm in greatest dimension

Metastases to Nonregional Lymph Nodes and/or Organs (M)

Mx	Distant metastasis cannot be assessed.
M0	No distant metastasis (no spread to lymph nodes outside the area of the tumor or to organs)
M1	Distant metastasis
M1a	Metastasis to nonregional lymph nodes or to the lung
M1b	Metastasis to organs such as liver, brain, and bone

Serum Tumor Markers (S)***

Sx	Marker studies not available or not performed
S0	Markers within normal limits
S1	$LDH > 1.5 \times N$ and $hCG > 5{,}000$ and $AFP > 1{,}000$
S2	$LDH\ 1.5\text{–}10 \times N$ or $hCG\ 5{,}000\text{–}50{,}000$ or $AFP\ 1{,}000\text{–}10{,}000$
S3	$LDH > 10 \times N$ or $hCG > 50{,}000$ or $AFP > 10{,}000$

   * The designation pT implies that the tumor (T) has been analyzed in the pathology laboratory.

  ** The designation pN implies that the lymph node (N) has been analyzed in the pathology laboratory.

*** LDH units: N, the upper limit of normal for the assay used; hCG units: milli international units (mIU)/mL; AFP units: ng/mL.

Source: Adapted from American Cancer Society, "Detailed Guide, Testicular Cancer: How is Testicular Cancer Staged?" http://www.cancer.org/docroot/CRI/content/CRI_2_4_3X_How_is_ testicular_cancer_staged_41.asp?sitearea= (accessed August 21, 2008). National Cancer Institute, "Testicular Cancer Treatment," http://www.cancer.gov/cancertopics/pdq/treatment/testicular/ HealthProfessional/page4 (accessed August 21, 2008); and A. Bahrami, J. Y. Ro, and A. G. Ayala, "An Overview of Testicular Germ Cell Tumors," *Archives of Pathology and Laboratory Medicine*, 131, 8 (2007): 1267–1280.

STAGE	PT (TUMOR)	N (N OR pN) (REGIONAL LYMPH NODES)	M (DISTANT METASTASIS)	S (SERUM TUMOR MARKERS)
I	pT1-4	N0	M0	Sx
IA	pT1	N0	M0	S0
IB	pT2-4	N0	M0	S0
IS	Any pT/Tx	N0	M0	S1-3
II	Any pT/Tx	N1-3	M0	Sx
IIA	Any pT/Tx	N1	M0	S0-1
IIB	Any pT/Tx	N2	M0	S0-1
IIC	Any pT/Tx	N3	M0	S0-1
III	Any pT/Tx	Any N	M1	Sx
IIIA	Any pT/Tx	Any N	M1a	S0-1
IIIB	Any pT/Tx	N1-3	M0	S2
	Any pT/Tx	Any N	M1a	S2
IIIC	Any pT/Tx	N1-3	M0	S3
	Any pT/Tx	Any N	M1a	S3
	Any pT/Tx	Any N	M1b	Any S

TABLE 7.2. STAGES OF TESTICULAR CANCER BASED ON GROUPING OF SERUM TUMOR MARKER (S) AND TNM CLASSIFICATION SYSTEM.

Adapted from American Cancer Society, "Detailed Guide, Testicular Cancer: How is Testicular Cancer Staged?" http://www.cancer.org/docroot/CRI/content/CRI_2_4_3X_How_is_testicular_cancer_staged_41.asp?sitearea= (accessed August 21, 2008); National Cancer Institute, "Testicular Cancer Treatment," http://www.cancer.gov/cancertopics/pdq/treatment/testicular/HealthProfessional/page4 (accessed August 21, 2008); and A. Bahrami, J.Y. Ro, and A. G. Ayala, "An Overview of Testicular Germ Cell Tumors," *Archives of Pathology and Laboratory Medicine*, 131, 8 (2007): 1267–1280.

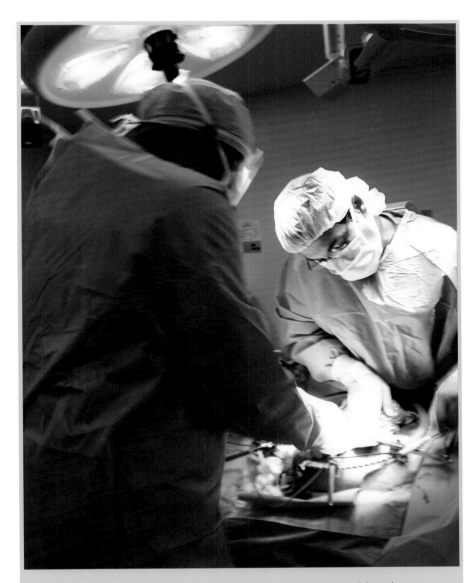

Figure 7.1   An orchiectomy followed by retroperitoneal lymph node dissection (RPLND)—surgical removal of the testicle and the retroperitoneal lymph nodes—can often cure testicular cancer if there has not been metastasis to the lungs or brain. In other cases this surgery can be used in combination with chemotherapy and/or radiation therapy. *(© Dr. Barry Slaven/Visuals Unlimited, Inc.)*

above (suprahilar) and below (infrahilar) where the ureters and blood vessels connect to the kidneys. In addition, a surgical technique used to reach lymph tissue from behind the aorta and the vena cava was introduced. One problem with the RPLND surgeries being done at that time was that removal of the suprahilar nodes led to some added surgical complications. Another problem was that, in the process of removing retroperitoneal lymph nodes, nerves that controlled ejaculation were often damaged. This resulted in sperm being ejaculated into the bladder rather than through the urethra (**retrograde ejaculation**), which rendered the patient infertile.

In the 1980s, physician John Donohue and his colleagues at Indiana University began to investigate whether they could safely reduce the number of lymph nodes removed in a RPLND in order to minimize surgical complications, including the nerve damage that caused retrograde ejaculation. To do this, they evaluated lymph nodes of many patients so they could map the common pathways of spread to the retroperitoneal nodes. As part of this study, they compared the metastasis patterns of right-sided and left-sided tumors. They found that for early stage testicular cancer, right-sided tumors metastasized to different sets of lymph nodes than left-sided tumors.

Based on this and other information, RPLND surgery began to change. The surgically complex removal of suprahilar lymph nodes could often be eliminated without increased risk of death from cancer. And, rather than performing a full bilateral dissection, surgeons began to perform modified—more unilateral—surgeries, with certain lymph nodes (mostly those on the left side of the retroperitoneum) removed for left-side tumors and others (mostly those on the right side) removed for right-side tumors. With fewer nodes removed, damage to nerves that are important to normal ejaculation was minimized. Did the change from bilateral RPLNDs to the more one-sided approach affect the success of the surgery? Initial studies suggested that there was no important effect. But Joel Sheinfeld of Memorial Sloan-Kettering Cancer Center in New York argues that without bilateral RPLND there is increased cancer risk to the patient. He supports his argument in part with a study that looked for metastasis to lymph nodes that were outside the normal areas used in many modified surgeries. They evaluated 500 patients who underwent RPLND for stage I and IIA nonseminomatous testicular cancer in the years 1989 to 2004. They found that up to 23 percent of those who had laboratory-verified metastasis to retroperitoneal lymph nodes had metastasis to retroperitoneal lymph nodes that that would not have been removed during modified RPLND.[4]

As more was learned about nerve control of ejaculation, surgical procedures were modified so that important nerve tissue could be pulled out of the way to prevent damage during lymph node removal. This further decreased the chances of retrograde ejaculation. This modified surgical procedure is known as nerve-sparing RPLND. The nerve-sparing surgical procedures for RPLND have evolved to the point where, even for stage II disease (when a bilateral RPLND is often performed), surgeons are still frequently able to preserve a man's ability to ejaculate normally. There are still some complex surgical situations, however, in which nerve function cannot be spared.

Traditional RPLND is an open surgery, meaning that the lymph nodes are accessed by opening the abdominal cavity with a long incision that runs down most of the abdomen. In 1992, surgeons from the University of Chicago reported on their use of a minimally invasive procedure to perform a RPLND. Only tiny holes had to be made to allow the insertion of surgical instruments. Because one of these instruments is an imaging tool known as a laparoscope, the procedure is referred to as **laparoscopic**

RPLND. An important benefit of the minimally invasive procedure, used by a growing number of physicians, is a reduction in surgical complications and a more rapid recovery time. Controversy remains, however, about whether it is as effective as open surgery in prevention of recurrence.

CHEMOTHERAPY

Testicular cancer, even after it has metastasized, typically responds well to chemotherapy—the use of chemicals to treat disease. Testicular cancer is more sensitive to chemotherapy than most cancers, although the reason for this is not understood.

Chemotherapy may be the sole postorchiectomy treatment, or it may be used in combination with other treatments such as RPLND. For seminoma patients, chemotherapy is most often used if there is a retroperitoneal lymph node mass greater than 5 centimeters (bulky retroperitoneal disease/stage IIC) or if the cancer has metastasized beyond the retroperitoneum (stage III). For nonseminoma patients, chemotherapy is used to treat bulky retroperitoneal disease and disease that has metastasized beyond the retroperitoneum; it is also a treatment option for nonbulky retroperitoneal disease (stages IIA and IIB).

Successful chemotherapy to treat testicular cancer began with the work of Min Chiu Li at Sloan-Kettering in the late 1950s, a time when chemotherapy as a treatment for cancer was in its infancy. Li had received his medical degree in China and was further trained in medicine and research after coming to the United States in 1947. Fresh from his success in using chemotherapy to cure gestational carcinoma in women, Li hoped that chemotherapy would also be effective against testicular cancer. He treated patients who had metastatic testicular cancer using a combination of three chemicals: dactinomycin (a chemical made by a bacterium); chlorambucil (a chemical related to the chemical warfare agent mustard gas); and methotrexate (a chemical that had been successfully used against leukemia in children and the one that Li had used against gestational choriocarcinoma).

In 1960, Li reported the results of his study: 50 percent of the patients responded to the chemotherapy and 10 to 20 percent of the patients responded with **complete remission (CR)**, meaning that no signs of cancer could be found.[5] CR is not the same as a cure, and some patients in remission eventually relapsed (their cancer returned). However, half of the CR patients did not relapse, meaning that 5 to 10 percent of those treated were cured. Given today's testicular cancer chemotherapy success rate, these numbers may appear grim, but as a first step the results were remarkable. As a result of Li's work, dactinomycin as **single-agent chemotherapy** or used with the other chemicals in combination chemotherapy became the treatment standard for disseminated testicular cancer until the mid-1970s.

Two new chemotherapy agents—vinblastine (a chemical derived from a plant) and bleomycin (a chemical derived from a bacterium)—were introduced several years later. These two drugs were tested in combination in testicular cancer patients by Melvin L. Samuels at The University of Texas M.D. Anderson Cancer Center in Houston in the early 1970s. Samuels found these two drugs acted synergistically—the effect of the two together was greater than would be expected by simply adding the success rates of each when used in single-agent chemotherapy. Most importantly, these patients did much better than patients receiving dactinomycin-based therapy: The CR rate was 57 percent, and most of these CR patients were cured.[6]

The discovery of the chemotherapy agent cisplatin by Barnett Rosenberg in 1965 set the stage for another leap forward. Following studies that showed cisplatin's success as single-agent chemotherapy and the vinblastine/bleomycin work of Samuels, Larry Einhorn at Indiana University treated patients using combination chemotherapy with vinblastine (V), bleomycin (B), and cisplatin (P)—(PVB)—in the mid-1970s. He achieved a CR rate of 70 percent with chemotherapy alone, and 11

◆ THE DISCOVERY OF CISPLATIN

The value of cisplatin—an inorganic compound containing the heavy metal platinum—to chemotherapy was discovered accidentally by Barnett Rosenberg at Michigan State University in 1965. During an experiment to examine the effect of an electrical field on bacteria, Rosenberg found that the reproductive process of the bacterium was affected. Instead of growing a bit longer and then dividing in two, the bacteria would grow to extremely long lengths (300 times normal) but not divide. He became intrigued, sought the assistance of colleagues in other disciplines, and soon discovered that the elongation was due not to the electric field but to a chemical that had been formed through interaction of the platinum electrodes used to create the electric field and the liquid medium in which the bacteria were suspended. That chemical was cisplatin, a previously known compound, cis-diamminedichloroplatinum or Peyrone's salt.

Rosenberg recognized that if cisplatin could affect bacterial division, it might also affect the division of cancer cells. Preclinical studies (laboratory studies done before patients are treated) showed it to be an effective antitumor agent, and clinical studies by Einhorn and others showed its effectiveness in testicular cancer patients.

percent more became disease-free following RPLND. Thus, a total of 81 percent became disease-free following treatment. Most importantly, 53 percent of the patients were cured.[7]

In the early 1980s, a large study was conducted by a group known as the Southeastern Cancer Study Group that compared PVB therapy to

Figure 7.2   Dr. Barnett Rosenberg discovered the chemotherapeutic properties of cisplatin. (© James L. Amos/Photo Researchers, Inc.)

therapy in which etoposide (E)—a chemical made from a plant product—was substituted for vinblastine; postchemotherapy RPLND was performed if possible when disease was found in the retroperitoneum following chemotherapy, and additional chemotherapy (PV only) was given if needed. Etoposide was selected because its effectiveness in combination with cisplatin had been shown in an earlier trial and to eliminate a side effect of vinblastine. The BEP group was shown to do better than the PVB group, with 83 percent and 74 percent becoming disease-free, respectively.[8]

Researchers continue to develop and evaluate new chemotherapy drugs and regimens, especially for patients whose prognosis is poor and those who cannot be cured by initial chemotherapy (**induction therapy**) and therefore need additional chemotherapy (**salvage therapy**). Today, most patients with metastatic testicular cancer whose prognosis is good and who are treated with induction chemotherapy receive three cycles of BEP therapy; because of bleomycin toxicity, some receive four cycles of EP instead. Intermediate- and poor-prognosis patients commonly receive four cycles of BEP as induction chemotherapy.

Patients who do not achieve CR—or who achieve CR and then relapse—are subsequently treated with a variety of regimens. Approaches include treatment with combination chemotherapy using ifosfamide—a drug related to chlorambucil, cisplatin, and either vinblastine, etoposide, or paclitaxel at standard dosages or treatment with high-dose chemotherapy. High-dose chemotherapy has most commonly involved treatment with etoposide and carboplatin. Since use of high doses of chemotherapy drugs destroys **hematopoietic**, or blood cell-producing, stem cells of the bone marrow, high-dose chemotherapy would normally be fatal. Doctors solve this problem by **stem cell rescue**—transfusion of hematopoietic stem cells that were harvested from the patient's own blood before the chemotherapy. These stem cells repopulate the bone marrow, where they divide repeatedly to maintain their own population and produce various blood cell types. Einhorn reviewed the cases of 184 patients whose salvage therapy involved high-dose chemotherapy and stem cell rescue. With post-treatment follow-up times ranging from 14 to 188 months (median 48 months), 116 of 184 patients (63 percent) were found to be in complete remission, an excellent success rate in this population.[9]

Testicular Cancer Chemotherapy from Plants

Three drugs used to treat testicular cancer—etoposide, vinblastine, and paclitaxel—are organic compounds that come from plants. Since plants have been used for medicinal purposes throughout history, it was a logical leap for scientists to evaluate plant extracts for their chemotherapeutic value.

Etoposide is made in the laboratory by modification of a chemical (podophyllotoxin) produced by plants in the genus *Podophyllum*: *P. emodi* Wall. (common name, Bankakri), which grows in the Himalayas of India and Nepal, and *P. peltatum* L. (American mayapple) which grows in eastern North America. For years, rhizome (underground stem) extracts from these toxic plants were used by indigenous peoples for medicinal purposes, such as remedying constipation. Extensive work on the purification and modification of active substances in extracts from these plants led to etoposide synthesis from podophyllotoxin by Hartmann Stähelin, a Swiss physician scientist, in the 1960s.

Vinblastine was isolated from the Madagascar periwinkle, *Catharanthus roseus*. For years, this plant was used by people in different parts of the world to treat a range of ailments. Canadian physician and researcher Robert Noble at the University of Western Ontario became curious about the medical properties of this plant after his brother sent him leaves from the plant and explained that they were used to make a Jamaican tea used in diabetes treatment. Noble tested extracts from the plant, but could find no effect on diabetes. He did find that it decreased the white blood cell count and thus reasoned that it might work against blood cell cancers. Biochemist Charles Thomas Beer joined Noble's lab and isolated the active compound, vinblastine, which proved in clinical trials to be an effective chemotherapeutic agent. Both Noble and Beer were inducted into the Canadian Medical Hall of Fame in recognition of their important work.

Testicular Cancer Therapy from Bacteria

Dactinomycin, an early testicular cancer chemotherapy agent, and bleomycin, used since the 1970s to treat testicular cancer, are organic compounds derived from fungus-like bacteria belonging to the actinomycetes group, genus *Streptomyces*.

Dactinomycin (Actinomycin D) was discovered in the 1940s by Selman Waxman, a soil microbiologist at Rutgers University. Waxman was especially interested in chemicals produced by soil bacteria. These microbe-produced chemicals intrigued him because some—which he termed **antibiotics**—would hinder other microbes and so could possibly be used to treat infectious diseases. Waxman discovered several of these compounds, including streptomycin, which successfully treated tuberculosis. Waxman was awarded the Nobel Prize in Physiology or Medicine for this work.

Some of the antibiotics Waxman discovered, such as dactinomycin, were effective against other microbes, but were too toxic for use in humans. Although disappointing from an infectious-disease viewpoint, it was recognized that some of these drugs might be able to kill cancer cells. This was found to be the case for dactinomycin, which was subsequently shown by Min Chiu Li to act against testicular cancer.

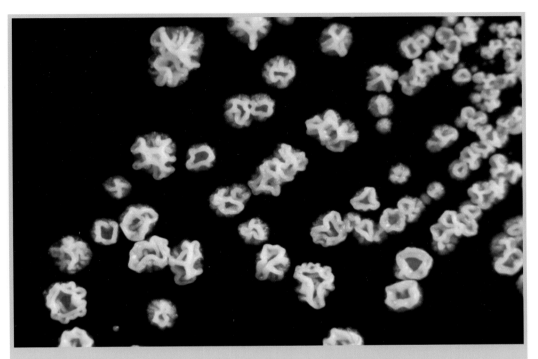

Figure 7.3 Bacteria of the genus *Streptomyces* are used to make antibiotics and chemotherapy drugs. Shown here is *Streptomyces* griseus, which is used to produce the antibiotic streptomycin. *(© Dr. Christine Case/Visuals Unlimited,*

Another microbiologist, Japanese physician Hamao Umezawa, was also interested in the chemicals produced by these soil bacteria. Umezawa grew many strains of the bacteria, filtered the medium in which each had grown, and evaluated the filtered media for ability to kill other microbes and cancer cells. Through this process, he discovered the chemotherapy agent bleomycin.

Why would soil bacteria produce chemicals that affect other microbes and cells in general? A commonly accepted explanation is that these chemicals help the bacteria compete with microbes in the environment, but scientists are exploring many other possibilities.

Mode of Action of Chemotherapeutic Agents

Chemotherapy chemicals work in a variety of ways to kill cells or prevent them from dividing. In some cases, the chemical does not directly kill the cell, but rather leads to changes that cause the cell to kill itself through a process known as **apoptosis**, a programmed series of events that lead to cell death. Vinblastine and paclitaxel prevent cell division by affecting microtubules, structures made of the protein tubulin that assemble and then disassemble to separate gene-bearing chromosomes during cell division. Vinblastine does this by preventing microtubule assembly, while paclitaxel hinders microtubule disassembly. Etoposide works by interfering with an enzyme (topoisomerase II) that helps to keep DNA, the cell's genetic material, from becoming knotted as it winds or unwinds to control cellular processes. The enzyme normally does this by making breaks in the DNA, which are then rapidly repaired. In the presence of etoposide, however, these DNA breaks are not rapidly repaired, resulting in permanent DNA damage. Cisplatin and bleomycin also cause DNA damage. There is still much to be learned about how bleomycin works to inhibit cancer cells, but it has been shown to bind—along with a metal such as iron—to DNA, causing breaks. Oxygen plays a role in the process, and it has been suggested that the bleomycin-metal complex causes oxygen to convert to toxic compounds, such as superoxide, which actually cause the DNA damage. Recently, researchers at Indiana University School of Medicine and Purdue University have produced three-dimensional images of bleomycin (with an attached metal) bound to DNA. Their hope is that a better understanding of how bleomycin interacts with DNA will help to find ways to improve bleomycin function.

CHEMOTHERAPY SIDE EFFECTS

Chemotherapy agents are by definition **cytotoxic**: They are toxic to cells. The benefit for cancer treatment is that these agents hinder the cancer cells. But there is a downside: The chemicals can also harm other cells in the body, causing unwanted effects. Some of these side effects, such as vomiting, can be reduced by other drugs. Problems can also be reduced by ensuring that the chemicals chosen for combination chemotherapy do not have the *same* toxicities, which would compound the problem. For example, bleomycin can cause lung inflammation (pneumonitis), and some individuals develop scar tissue in the lungs (pulmonary fibrosis), which can be fatal. Yet because it is does not cause myelosupression, the depression of blood cell production by the bone marrow, bleomycin can be combined with a drug such as etoposide that does.

RADIATION THERAPY

The use of radiation to treat cancer is a commonly used postorchiectomy treatment for stage I and IIA-B seminoma patients. It is not used as a treatment for nonseminoma patients because, for reasons that are not known, nonseminoma is less sensitive to radiation than is seminoma.

Radiation therapy, unlike chemotherapy, has the advantage of targeting the treatment to a particular area of the body. Because seminoma metastasizes in a predictable fashion, radiation targets the regional lymph nodes.

For testicular cancer, the patient lies on a table and areas of the body to be protected from radiation, especially the remaining testicle, are protected by a shield. Radiation is an external-beam process, which means that a machine outside the body sends a high-power energy beam (e.g. X-rays) into the body. The machine can rotate so that the patient is irradiated from different angles.

Care is managed by a radiation oncologist who determines the fields (areas) to be irradiated, the total dosage (rads), and the number of days over which treatments are given. The radiation dosage needed for successful treatment of testicular cancer is low compared to some other cancers.

Radiation works by damaging cellular DNA. The cancer cells are generally more sensitive to radiation than healthy cells. This is because healthy cells can often repair the radiation-induced damage done to them in between treatments. There are negative side effects to radiation therapy, however, such as diarrhea, nausea, vomiting, and fatigue. The skin in the irradiated area may become red and sensitive, similar to sunburn. Infertility is usually temporary, but may last for one to two years.

SURVEILLANCE

For some patients in the earliest stage of testicular cancer, no treatment beyond the orchiectomy is planned. Instead, these patients may undergo surveillance. Surveillance involves the monitoring of the patient's blood work and the use of imaging techniques to look for signs of a relapse and providing additional treatment only if surveillance shows a recurrence. For those patients who elect surveillence and do not have a recurrence, the benefit is clear: They will avoid the risks associated with additional treatments.

SUMMARY

The treatment for testicular cancer depends largely on the type of testicular cancer a patient has and the cancer stage. For testicular cancer, if the cancer is localized to the testis or nearby structures, the patient is considered to be in stage I. Stage II means that the cancer has spread to regional lymph nodes (mostly commonly retroperitoneal lymph nodes). Stage III means that the cancer has spread to distant locations beyond the regional nodes. The first treatment step for all is the orchiectomy. In some stage I patients, the orchiectomy is the only treatment and patients are carefully monitored for relapse and given additional treatment only in the event of a relapse. In most cases, additional treatment is used. Treatment options include retroperitoneal lymph node dissection, chemotherapy, and radiation therapy. Radiation therapy is only used for seminoma patients, as nonseminoma does not respond well to this treatment.

8

WHAT CAUSES TESTICULAR CANCER?

KEY POINTS

♦ Testicular cancer most likely occurs as the result of a combination of genetic and environmental factors, but the causes are not yet known.

♦ Environmental factors suspected of playing a role in testicular cancer development include those of the intrauterine environment to which a male is exposed during fetal life.

♦ Some occupations, such as firefighting, appear to increase the risk of testicular cancer development.

♦ Established risk factors for testicular cancer are cryptorchidism and having a family member with testicular cancer. Also, men who have had cancer in one testicle are at increased risk of developing cancer in the other testicle.

♦ Testicular cancer rates are higher in some parts of the world than others. In the United States, white men are at greater risk of testicular cancer than African American men.

THE LEATHER TANNERS

Gloversville is one of the "Glove Cities" of Fulton County, New York, so named for their prominent role in leather glove manufacturing and leather tanning in the nineteenth and twentieth centuries. In a three-year period in the 1980s, three "Glove City" tanners were diagnosed with testicular cancer. Their cases are summarized in the *Morbidity and Mortality Weekly Report*, a Centers for Disease Control and Prevention publication: "The first case occurred in 1982, when embryonal carcinoma was diagnosed in a 31-year-old worker who had begun work in leather tanning 13 years earlier. A second case of combined seminoma and embryonal carcinoma was diagnosed in 1984 in a 36-year-old worker who had begun work in this industry 19 years earlier. The third case of embryonal carcinoma was also diagnosed in 1984 in a 25-year-old worker who had worked in tanning for 8 years."[1]

These three men had more in common than the type of testicular cancer and their employment history with Fulton County tanneries: They had all been employed by Gloversville's Pan American Tannery during the same time period, on the same shift, and in the same area of the same department—the spray line of the leather-finishing department. The spray line involved conveyor belts that moved tanned hides past dye-depositing spray guns and then to swabbers who spread the dye onto the leather. Two of the men were swabbers and the other was a foreman whose job included cleaning spray guns and working as swabber. This cancer cluster was first reported in the journal *Lancet*. Stephen Levin and colleagues described the spray line: "The men had to lean over the hide, with their faces close to the leather. They wore no gloves and contamination of the skin and clothing by liquid dye was virtually continuous. During spray-line operations, a fine mist was present in the air, accompanied by a strong, solvent-like odor, which was said to be detectable up to 200 meters from the tannery. General ventilation was provided only by windows; these were usually kept open, except in winter."[2]

Why did these men develop testicular cancer? Was it related to their job, or were the similarities in their work histories simply a coincidence? After all, tannery work was a common occupation in Fulton County, so even if testicular cancer were to occur at a "normal" rate, it is not a surprise that tanners in the county would be affected. It is usually not possible to determine with certainty the cause of a given person's cancer, but a partial answer to the cause question comes from statistical analyses that showed the testicular cancer rate among Pan American finishing department workers to be significantly greater than the expected rate, which was derived from actual testicular cancer rates in males from up-state New York. If their cancers were related to their jobs at the tannery, did these men have other risk factors that increased their chances of getting cancer? After all, there were many men employed in their department who did not develop testicular cancer. If it was job related, what chemicals or other work conditions were responsible? This question is nearly impossible to answer on a case-by-case basis. The men had been exposed to many chemicals, and as a further complication, two of the men had worked previously on spray lines at other tanneries.

In the Levin report, speculation surrounded the solvent dimethylformamide (DMF). One of the reasons for singling out DMF was because it had been suspected in other testicular cancer clusters, including two at aircraft maintenance facilities. Suspicion is not proof, however, and the cause of testicular cancer in these men remains uncertain.

ENVIRONMENT, GENETICS, AND TESTICULAR CANCER

The incidence of testicular cancer has increased in recent decades: In the past five decades, the incidence has more than doubled. This

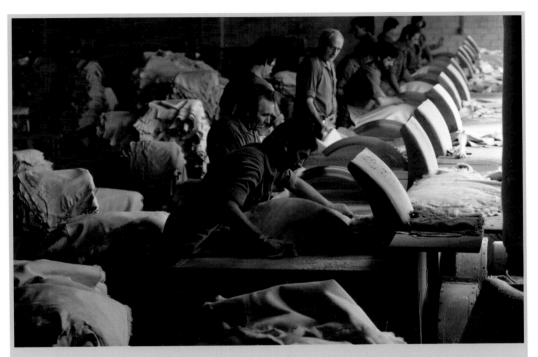

Figure 8.1 Tannery workers, such as those shown here, are at a higher risk for testicular cancer. Exposure to dimethylformamide (DMF), a chemical solvent used in tanneries, is suspected to be to blame for this increased risk, although it has not been proven conclusively. *(© Stephanie Maze/CORBIS)*

increase in occurrence suggests that the environment plays an important role in testicular cancer development; while a person's genetic makeup undoubtedly plays a role, genetics alone would not account for these recent increases.

The study on the leather tanners suggests a role for environmental factors such as chemical pollutants, but many questions persist. If environmental factors play a role in testicular cancer, what other environmental factors might be involved? Can radiation play a role? Can particular microorganisms infect a person and contribute, directly or indirectly, to development of this cancer? Since testicular cancer typically develops early in life, can the intrauterine environment to which the developing fetus is exposed (e.g., toxicants, normal maternal chemicals such as hormones) play a role? Can a person's own hormonal environment influence testicular cancer development? To what extent is a person's hormonal environment influenced by factors in the external environment? Researchers continue to examine testicular cancer data in an attempt to identify relevant environmental factors for testicular cancer development. The task is challenging for many reasons, which include the small size of the pool of affected individuals, the fact that testicular cancer is not a single disease, and that analysis typically begins only after a diagnosis of testicular cancer has been made.

Studies have attempted to uncover links between testicular cancer and other factors, such as maternal age, but without success. An intriguing question arose about diethylstilbestrol (DES), a synthetic estrogen prescribed to many pregnant women between the late 1930s and early 1970s to prevent miscarriage. Sons of women who took DES during pregnancy could be at greater risk for testicular cancer. Many different investigations looked into this question. While it has been shown that DES daughters are at increased risk of a type of vaginal/cervical cancer and reproductive abnormalities, the only clearly demonstrated effect on DES sons is an increased risk for epididymal cysts, which are benign. It has not been established that DES sons are at increased risk of testicular cancer; some studies have shown that DES sons are at increased risk, while others have not shown a DES-testicular cancer relationship.

Katherine McGlynn and colleagues at the NCI have recently found evidence of a link between DDT, a pesticide now banned in the United States, and testicular GCTs. Their study took advantage of the fact that hundreds of U.S. servicemen had given blood samples well before any of them developed testicular cancer. These blood samples were still available and could be evaluated to see if any chemicals in them might be linked to later development of testicular cancer. The researchers found that those who had high concentrations of a DDT breakdown product in their blood were significantly more likely to eventually develop testicular cancer than those with low concentrations. DDT and other organochlorine (organic compounds with chlorine) pesticides have long been suspected in testicular cancer because they can affect hormones in the body, which themselves have been suspected to influence the risk of this cancer.

Another way to assess environmental factors is to examine occupational risk—whether certain occupations (such as leather tanning) carry increased testicular cancer risk. For example, many studies show that firefighters are at increased risk for testicular cancers due to their occupational exposure to soot and chemicals such as benzene. (British Columbia now defines testicular cancer as an occupational risk for firefighters.) Another study suggested that the use of handheld radar guns by police (often positioned near testicles) might increase testicular cancer risk. Many other occupations have also been evaluated.

What is the role of genetics? A known, established risk factor for testicular cancer is a family history of testicular cancer. The greatest risk is having a brother with testicular cancer, which increases the risk up to tenfold, more than is normally seen with other cancers. This suggests an important role for genetics in the development of testicular cancer. (It is important to remember, however, that brothers often have numerous environmental factors in common.) If a gene or genes play a role, on what chromosomes are these susceptibility genes located? Studies to find regions of chromosomes that may affect testicular cancer risk rely on analysis of affected families, defined as families with two

Figure 8.2   The pesticide DDT was widely used in the first half of the twentieth century. In this photograph an army field hospital is being sprayed with DDT. It was later discovered that exposure to DDT led to an elevated risk of testicular cancer. (© *National Library of Medicine/U.S. Institutes of Health*)

or more individuals with testicular cancer. For testicular cancer, such studies are limited by the small number of affected families. To date, no studies have conclusively pointed to a specific chromosome region as associated with testicular cancer development. More likely, testicular cancer risk is influenced by many genes scattered throughout a person's chromosomes.

If scientists do eventually find genes associated with testicular cancer, this will not rule out a role for the environment. Most likely, testicular cancer will be found to be caused by a combination of environmental and genetic factors.

ESTABLISHED RISK FACTORS FOR TESTICULAR CANCER

In addition to a family history of testicular cancer, there are two other known risk factors: cryptorchidism (undescended testicle) and a personal history of testicular cancer.

Up to 5 percent of boys are born with cryptorchidism. Men who have a history of cryptorchidism have a testicular cancer risk that is 2 to 8 times the normal rate. For most of those born with cryptorchidism, the testicle descends spontaneously into the scrotum within a few months of birth. However, for the remainder the testicle does not descend on its own, and treatment (commonly with **orchiopexy**, a surgery that places the testicle in the scrotum) is warranted. The age at which this surgery is performed varies, but many urologists now recommend surgery before the age of one year. Orchiopexy is important for eventual sperm production; relative to testicular cancer, it allows for a testicular abnormality—such as a lump—to be felt, increasing the likelihood of early detection.

Since cryptorchidism increases the chance of testicular cancer, can the risk of developing testicular cancer risk be reduced by orchiopexy? If so, does the age at which orchiopexy occurs affect this risk? A study of close to 17,000 men in Sweden compared the testicular cancer risk in those who underwent orchiopexy before the age of 13 to those who had surgery at 13 years or older (approximately pre- vs. postpuberty) and found that early surgery halved the risk.[3] However, a similar study in Denmark showed that orchiopexy age had no effect on testicular cancer risk.[4]

Why is cryptorchidism a risk factor for testicular cancer? Could it be because it can somehow cause testicular cancer? Alternatively, could cryptorchidism and testicular cancer have the same cause or causes? The answers to these questions are not yet known. The path to the answer will likely be influenced by an interesting fact: The increased testicular cancer risk extends to the normally descended testicle as well as to the cryptorchid testis.

A personal history of testicular cancer is a risk factor for testicular cancer. In other words, a person who develops testicular cancer is at increased risk for developing testicular cancer in the other (contralateral) testicle. Sometimes the two cancers occur simultaneously, but often the second cancer occurs later. These second cancers are primary cancers and are not due to metastasis. Men who have been treated for testicular cancer are informed of the risk to the other testicle so they can be alert to symptoms, and the other testicle is carefully evaluated during follow-up exams.

TESTICULAR CANCER RATES VARY AMONG DIFFERENT GROUPS

In the United States, testicular cancer occurs more frequently in white men than in African American men—some reports say the rate is up to 5 times higher. It is also more frequent in white men than in Asian, Pacific Islander, or Alaska Native men. The incidence is lower for Hispanic white men than non-Hispanic white men

In addition, testicular cancer rates are not uniform across the globe. There is a high incidence of testicular cancer in Scandinavian countries, Germany, and New Zealand. The lowest rates are in Asia and Africa. It is not known why this is the case, but, interestingly, this increased risk does not appear to disappear when people from these parts of the world migrate to different places.

SUMMARY

The causes of testicular cancer are not known, but it most likely occurs as a result of a combination of environmental and genetic factors. Since testicular cancer tends to occur at a young age, scientists are particularly interested in determining the role of the intrauterine environment in testicular cancer development. The intrauterine environment includes truly external factors such as toxicants as well as more internal factors, such as hormones produced by the mother. Certain occupations may put a person at greater risk of developing testicular cancer. A man is more likely to develop testicular cancer if he has a family member, particularly a brother, who developed testicular cancer and if he was born with an undescended testicle. Another risk factor for testicular cancer is testicular cancer itself: A man who develops testicular cancer has an increased chance of developing a new testicular cancer in the other testicle. Testicular cancer rates are greater in some parts of the world than other. In the United States, testicular cancer occurs at a greater rate in white men than in African American men.

9

CHALLENGES AND QUESTIONS FOR THE FUTURE

KEY POINTS

- Despite the remarkable progress that has been made in the field of testicular cancer, many questions and challenges remain.

- Most men survive testicular cancer, but better success is needed to help those whose initial prognosis is poor or those who do not respond successfully to initial treatment.

- Physicians want to be able to minimize the treatment needed for testicular cancer while maintaining the current success rate.

- Researchers want to learn more about the many steps that occur as a normal cell of the testicle is transformed into a cancer cell, and they want to understand why, and when, these changes occur.

- Physicians and researchers from a variety of training backgrounds can contribute to the field of testicular cancer research.

There have been remarkable successes in the diagnosis and treatment of testicular cancer, but important and exciting challenges remain. Some of these challenges are at the clinical level where they most affect patient survival. Some are at the environmental level where solutions may eventually prevent some testicular cancers from developing. Other challenges are at the molecular level, where solutions may explain the many changes that occur in a cell as it is transformed to a cancer cell. Answers to molecular questions are interesting from a broad range of scientific perspectives, and they will ultimately help in the battle against testicular cancer.

DIAGNOSIS OF TESTICULAR CANCER

One of the challenges for the pathologist is the determination of testicular cancer type, as some can resemble others. In addition, for mixed GCTs, it is important that all tumor subtypes be identified. Immunohistochemistry, which can detect molecules specific to certain tumor cell types, has provided an important tool to pathologists. As scientists learn more about which molecules are specific to certain tumor cell types, the ability of immunohistochemistry to fine-tune diagnosis will increase.

TREATMENT OPTIONS

Advances in testicular cancer treatment make testicular cancer one of the most curable cancers. In some situations, such as stage I seminoma, the cure rate is close to 100 percent. Yet each year in the United States, hundreds of men die of testicular cancer; much of the effort to develop new treatment methods is therefore directed at this group. Some non-GCTs still carry a poor prognosis, and successful efforts are needed to address these rare cancers. Even for GCTs, with an overall cure rate of greater than 90 percent, the cure rate is lower (approximately 80 percent) once the disease has metastasized. For GCTs, more progress needs to be made in certain poor-risk categories: patients who relapse later than normal (two years post-therapy), patients with primary mediastinal non-seminomatous GCTs, teratoma patients whose tumors have undergone malignant transformation to form aggressive neural ectodermal tumors, and patients in need of salvage therapy.

The remarkable successes with chemotherapy and radiation in testicular cancer treatment bring another problem: long-term side effects, such as second cancers. While radiation and chemotherapy always bring such risks, the concern is greater for the typical testicular cancer patient because his young age at treatment increases the post-treatment years during which a new cancer can develop. These problems are being addressed in several ways. New chemotherapy and radiation protocols are being evaluated. In addition, for certain low-risk patients, surveillance rather than therapy is the preferred choice.

Surveillance carries obvious benefits, as those whose orchiectomy is followed only by monitoring will not experience the side effects of chemotherapy or radiation therapy. Surveillance addresses the problem that many low-risk patients can be cured by orchiectomy alone and so for these individuals, chemotherapy or radiation is over-treatment. The obvious dilemma that follows from this is that it is not currently possible on a case-by-case basis to predict which patients will *not* develop metastases. There is some information in this area; for example, it has been shown for stage I seminoma, larger primary tumors are more likely to metastasize than smaller ones. If metastasis potential based on tumor characteristics at the cellular or molecular level can be determined, individual treatment decisions will be easier. Whatever treatment changes are made, it is important that they do not compromise the existing successes. This is also true for RPLND, where debate is ongoing over minimally invasive versus open surgery, and on the surgical templates themselves.

GROWING UNDERSTANDING OF TESTICULAR CANCER

Researchers want to understand completely the steps by which a normal cell becomes a testicular cancer cell. For GCTs, progress has been made in this area, but many questions remain. Scientists have found that for postpuberty GCTs other than spermatocytic seminoma, GCTs are preceded by **carcinoma in situ**, which appears to always develop into a GCT. Interestingly, carcinoma in situ and GCTs share another common feature: They have extra DNA from a particular region of chromosome number 12. Sometimes this genetic material exists as an abnormal independent chromosome piece known as an **isochromosome**, at other times it is attached to an existing chromosome, but it is always present, suggesting that certain genes in this region are important in cancer development. Additional GCT characteristics that scientists want to learn more about are the presence of extra chromosomes (postpuberty GCTs often have three or four sets of chromosomes rather than two) and the loss of certain chromosome regions.

An interesting question surrounds the relationship among GCT types. The differences between pre- and postpuberty GCTs (for example, extra chromosome 12 material is not characteristic of prepuberty GCTs) are a curiosity, as is the difference in age profile between seminoma and nonseminoma patients. Scientists want to understand the relationship between carcinoma in situ and the various GCT types and whether each GCT type arises directly from carcinoma in situ or whether some GCT types develop from other GCT types.

Chemotherapy questions at the cellular level remain. Testicular cancer cells are generally more sensitive that other cancer cells to cisplatin, but scientists want to understand the underlying reason for this. They are also particularly interested in understanding the reasons that, for some men, testicular cancers do not respond to cisplatin. If the reasons for the lack of cisplatin sensitivity can be found, then hopefully those whose cancer will not respond can be identified before cisplatin therapy failure.

OPPORTUNITIES IN TESTICULAR CANCER RESEARCH

Testicular cancer research, which can take place in a clinical setting with patients, in the laboratory setting with animals or cells or molecules, and through computer analysis of cancer data, is an exciting field. Researchers come from a variety of backgrounds: Some are physicians (M.D., D.O.), some hold higher degrees (e.g., Ph.D.) in various scientific fields, some hold dual degrees (M.D./Ph.D.; Ph.D./MPH). They may differ in the academic areas in which they have trained. Some have studied molecular biology; others have focused in areas such as immunology, genetics, molecular biology, developmental biology, or epidemiology; and most have training that encompasses several disciplines. Physicians may differ in the areas in which they specialize. Some have trained in urology; others have trained in areas such as radiation oncology. All of these individuals are important to improved understanding of the causes of testicular cancer and improving treatment success.

SUMMARY

Many interesting questions and challenges remain regarding testicular cancer. The most important of these include improving treatment for

Figure 9.1   Doctors and researchers across many medical and science disciplines are working to improve our understanding of testicular cancer. *(© Radu Razvan/Shutterstock images)*

the testicular cancer types and cases that still carry a poor prognosis, and learning about the many cellular and molecular changes that occur as a normal cell of the testicle is transformed into a cancer cell. These challenges can be overcome by the work of individuals from a variety of academic and clinical backgrounds.

NOTES

◆

Chapter 1

1. Lawrence H. Einhorn, "Testicular Cancer: An Oncological Success Story," *Clinical Cancer Research* 3, 12 (1997): 2630–2632.

Chapter 2

1. Mike Eisenbath, "Jason's Story," http://www.testicularcancer.org/abouttcstoryone.htm (accessed August 21, 2008).
2. Sean Kimerling Testicular Cancer Foundation, "Survivor Stories," http://www.seankimerling.org/pages/programs/programs_videos_survivor.html (accessed August 21, 2008).
3. Tom Struble, "A Father's Challenge to Educators and the Medical Community," Jason A. Struble Memorial Cancer Fund, http://www.testicularcancer.org/ourchallenge-educators.htm (accessed August 21, 2008).

Chapter 7

1. American Cancer Society, "Detailed Guide, Testicular Cancer: How is Testicular Cancer Staged?" http://www.cancer.org/docroot/CRI/content/CRI_2_4_3X_How_is_testicular_cancer_staged_41.asp?sitearea= (accessed August 21, 2008).
2. National Cancer Institute, "Testicular Cancer Treatment," http://www.cancer.gov/cancertopics/pdq/treatment/testicular/HealthProfessional/page4 (accessed August 21, 2008).
3. A. Bahrami, Jae Y. Ro, and Alberto G. Ayala, "An Overview of Testicular Germ Cell Tumors," *Archives of Pathology and Laboratory Medicine* 131, 8 (2007): 1267–1280.
4. S. E. Eggener, B. S. Carver, D. S. Sharp, R. J. Motzer, G. J. Bosl, and J. Sheinfeld, "Incidence of Disease Outside Modified Retroperitoneal Lymph Node Dissection Templates in Clinical Stage I or IIA Nonseminomatous Germ Cell Testicular Cancer," *Journal of Urology* 177, 3 (2007): 937–943.
5. M. C. Li, W. F. Whitmore Jr., R. Golbey, and H. Grabstald, "Effects of Combined Drug Therapy on Metastatic Cancer of the Testis," *Journal of the American Medical Association* 174 (1960): 1291–1299.

6. M. L. Samuels, V. J. Lanzotti, P. Y. Holoye, L. E. Boyle, T. L. Smith, and D. E. Johnson, "An Update of the Velban-Bleomycin Program in Testicular Neoplasia with a Note on Cis-dichlorodiammineplatinum," *Cancer of the Genitourinary Tract*. New York: Raven Press, 1979, 159–172.

7. L. H. Einhorn, "Testicular Cancer: An Oncological Success Story," *Clinical Cancer Research* 3, 12 (1997): 2630–2632.

8. S. D. Williams, R. Birch, L. Irwin, A. Greco, P. J. Loehrer, and L. E. Einhorn, "Disseminated Germ Cell Tumors: Chemotherapy with Cisplatin Plus Bleomycin Plus either Vinblastine or Etoposide," *New England Journal of Medicine* 316 (1987): 1435–1440.

9. Lawrence H. Einhorn, Stephen D. Williams, Amy Chamness, Mary Brames, Susan Perkins, and Rafat Abonour, "High-Dose Chemotherapy and Stem-Cell Rescue for Metastatic Germ-Cell Tumors," *The New England Journal of Medicine* 357, 4 (2007): 340–348.

Chapter 8

1. Centers for Disease Control and Prevention, "Epidemiologic and Reports Testicular Cancer in Leather Workers—Fulton County, New York," *Morbidity and Mortality Weekly Report* 38, 7 (1989): 111–114.

2. S. M. Levin, D. B. Baker, P. J. Landrigan, S. V. Monaghan, E. Frumin, M. Braithwaite, and W. Towne, "Testicular Cancer in Leather Tanners Exposed to Dimethylformamide (letter)," *Lancet* 2, 8568 (1987): 1153.

3. A. Petterson, L. Richiardi, A. Nordenskjold, M. Kaijser, and O. Akre, "Age of Surgery for Undescended Testis and Risk of Testicular Cancer," *The New England Journal of Medicine* 356, 18 (2007): 1835–1841.

4. C. Myrup, et al., "Correction of Cryptorchidism and Testicular Cancer (correspondence)," *The New England Journal of Medicine* 357 (2007): 825–827.

GLOSSARY

♦

alpha-fetoprotein A protein normally made in fetal life that can be found at high concentrations in the blood of those with some types of testicular cancer.

antibiotic An antimicrobial compound produced by a microbe.

antibody A defensive protein that can bind specifically to other molecules.

apoptosis Programmed cell death.

blood-testis barrier A physical barrier formed by Sertoli cell junctions that prevents materials from passing between the blood and the cells of the testis.

cancer stage The degree to which a cancer has advanced.

carcinoma in situ An early cancer that has not invaded surrounding tissues.

chemotherapy The use of chemicals to treat cancer.

choriocarcinoma A type of nonseminomatous germ cell testicular cancer.

chorion A membrane associated with the embryo that forms the fetal part of the placenta.

clinical stage The cancer stage determined before tissue is removed and analyzed in a pathology laboratory.

complete remission The disappearance of all signs of a cancer.

computed tomography (CT) scan An imaging technique that uses X-rays to produce a three-dimensional image.

cryptorchidism A condition in which a testicle does not descend into the scrotum before birth.

cytotoxic Toxic to cells.

cytotrophoblasts Cells derived from trophoblasts that are part of the chorion.

diploid Having two copies of each chromosome.

efferent ductules Tubes that carry sperm from the testis to the epididymis.

ejaculatory duct A sperm-carrying tube (the end of each vas deferens) that joins the urethra.

embryonal carcinoma A type of nonseminomatous germ cell testicular cancer.

endocrine gland A group of cells that secrete materials directly into the bloodstream.

enzyme A protein that speeds up a chemical reaction but is not itself changed by the reaction.

epidemiologist A scientist who studies epidemiology, a science that examines the distribution and causes of disease.

epididymis A long, coiled tube that carries sperm from the efferent ductules that leave the testis to the vas deferens.

exocrine gland A group of cells that secrete materials through a duct.

external inguinal ring The end of the inguinal canal closest to the scrotum.

extraembryonic membranes Structures, such as the yolk sac, that are attached to an embryo and assist in its development.

extragonadal germ cell tumors Germ cell tumors that arise outside of the gonads.

gametes Reproductive cells (in males, sperm).

germ cell Gametes, or cells that develop into gametes.

germ cell cancer   A cancer of a cell that would normally develop into a germ cell.

germinal epithelium   The part of the seminiferous tubule dedicated to sperm production, i.e., the germ cells and the Sertoli cells.

gonads   Organs that form gametes (in males, the testes).

gonocytes   Cells in the embryo/fetus that are precursors of spermatogonia.

gubernaculum   The tissue that connects the testis to the inside of the scrotum.

gynecomastia   Enlargement of breast tissue in males.

haploid   Having one copy of each chromosome.

hematopoietic   Blood cell forming.

hilus   The region of a testis where blood, lymphatic, and sperm-carrying vessels connect.

histology   The microscopic study of tissues.

hormone   A substance made by one part of the body that travels through the blood to another and affects its activity.

human chorionic gonadotropin   A small protein hormone normally produced by the placenta to maintain pregnancy, which can be found at high concentration in the blood of those with some types of testicular cancer.

hydrocele   Fluid accumulation in a sac that surrounds the testicle.

immunohistochemistry   The use of antibodies to specifically label certain cellular molecules.

induction therapy   Initial chemotherapy.

inguinal canals   Tubelike passageways that connect the abdomen to the scrotum.

internal inguinal ring The end of an inguinal canal that is furthest from the scrotum.

interstitium An area of connective tissue that separates the seminiferous tubules of the testes.

isochromosome An abnormal chromosome, formed by abnormal chromosome division, with two identical arms (ends).

laparoscopic RPLND A type of retroperitoneal lymph node dissection performed using minimally invasive surgery in which the retroperitoneal lymph nodes are accessed by tiny incisions, one of which is used to insert a visualization instrument known as a laparoscope.

Leydig cells Cells of the interstitium of the testes that produce testosterone.

lobules Sections of the testes separated by connective tissue.

lymph Tissue fluid contained in lymph vessels.

lymph nodes Small organs located along lymphatic vessels that filter lymph and destroy, or become activated to destroy, microbes and cancer cells.

lymph vessels The tubes that collect excess tissue fluid and return it to the circulatory system.

malignant tumor A tumor that spreads to nearby tissues and may spread to more distant sites by metastasis (cancer).

mediastinum An area of the chest between the lungs.

mediastinum testis An area of the testis that is rich in connective tissue and contains the rete testis.

meiosis A type of cell division process that in animals produces haploid cells, or cells with only one copy of each chromosome (sperm in males).

metastasize   To spread from the site of the original tumor to other parts of the body.

mitosis   A type of cell division that produces cells identical to the parent cell.

mixed germ cell tumor   A type of germ cell tumor that contains more than one type of germ cell tumor.

neoplasm   A tumor, either benign or malignant.

non–germ cell cancer   A cancer of a cell of the gonad (testis in the male) that is not in the gamete (sperm in the male) developmental pathway.

nonseminoma   A type of germ cell tumor that includes embryonal carcinoma, yolk sac tumor, trophoblastic tumors such as choriocarcinoma, teratoma, and mixed germ cell tumors.

orchiectomy   A surgical procedure to remove a testicle.

orchiopexy   A surgical procedure to move an undescended testicle into the scrotum.

orchitis   Inflammation of the testis.

pampiniform plexus   Network of veins in the spermatic cord.

pathologic stage   The cancer stage as determined by tissue analyzed in a pathology laboratory.

pathologist   A physician who studies tissues to determine the presence and extent of disease.

peritoneum   The lining of the abdominal cavity.

placenta   The structure that connects and exchanges materials between the fetus and the mother.

primary spermatocytes   Cells in the sperm developmental pathway produced from spermatogonia that divide to produce secondary spermatocytes.

primordial germ cells   Cells in the developing embryo/fetus that are the precursors of gonocytes.

radiation therapy   The use of radiation to kill cancer cells.

radiologist   A physician who specializes in the use of radiation therapy.

rete testis   A network of tubules that collect sperm made by seminiferous tubules in the testis.

retrograde ejaculation   Movement of sperm into the bladder rather than the urethra.

retroperitoneal lymph node dissection (RPLND)   Removal of lymph nodes from the retroperitoneum.

retroperitoneum   An area at the back of the abdomen behind the peritoneum.

risk factor   Something that increases the chance of developing a disease.

salvage therapy   Treatment used after a cancer has failed to respond to initial treatments.

secondary spermatocytes   Cells in the sperm developmental pathway produced from primary spermatocytes that in turn produce spermatids.

semen   The sperm and seminal fluid released from the urethra during ejaculation.

seminal fluid   Fluid added to sperm in the vas deferens and urethra.

seminiferous tubules   Small tubes in the testes that produce sperm.

seminoma   A type of germ cell cancer.

Sertoli cells   Cells of the testis that assist in sperm development.

serum   The fluid portion of the blood that remains after blood coagulates.

single agent chemotherapy   Treatment of cancer with a single chemical agent.

somatic cells   Body cells that are not germ cells.

spermatic cord   The cord that suspends the testis in the scrotum and provides connections to the abdomen.

spermatids   Cells derived from secondary spermatocytes that in turn develop into sperm cells.

spermatocele   A fluid-filled cyst in the epididymis.

spermatocytic seminoma   A type of germ cell cancer that develops in older men.

spermatogenesis   The stepwise process of sperm formation.

spermatogonia   Spermatogenic stem cells that can divide to make copies of themselves and to primary spermatocytes that will develop into sperm.

spermiogenesis   Maturation of a spermatid into a sperm.

stem cell rescue   Infusion of bone marrow stem cells to replace those killed through chemotherapy.

syncytiotrophoblasts   Cells derived from trophoblasts that are part of the chorion.

teratoma   A type of nonseminomatous germ cell testicular cancer.

testicular torsion   Twisting of the spermatic cord resulting in loss of blood supply to the testicle.

testosterone   A steroid sex hormone produced largely by the testes that functions in the development and maintenance of male secondary sexual characteristics.

tissue fluid   Fluid that surrounds and bathes tissues of the body.

TNM system   A system used for cancer staging that evaluates the local spread of the primary tumor (T), its metastasis to regional lymph nodes (N), and its metastasis to nonregional lymph nodes and organs (M).

trophoblastic tumor   A type of nonseminomatous germ cell testicular cancer.

trophoblasts   Cells of the chorion.

tumor   An abnormal mass of cells produced by cell division (neoplasm), which can be benign or malignant.

tumor markers   Molecules whose presence or increased concentration in the blood or other tissues can indicate particular cancer types.

tunica albuginea   A smooth layer of connective tissue that forms the outside layer of a testicle.

tunica vaginalis   A flattened sac that wraps around much of a testis.

ultrasound   A diagnostic procedure that uses sound waves to analyze tissue.

urethra   A tube that carries sperm and urine to the outside of the body.

varicocele   An enlargement of the veins that carry blood from the testis.

vas deferens   A tube that carries sperm from the epididymis to the urethra.

X-ray   A type of radiation used for disease diagnosis.

yolk sac   An extraembryonic membrane that is responsible for production of a fetus's first blood cells and primordial germ cells.

BIBLIOGRAPHY

◆

Abrams, Dan. "Battling Testicular Cancer." *MSNBC*. September 9, 2004. Available online. URL: http://www.msnbc.msn.com/id/5952314. Accessed October 9, 2007.

Al-Agha, Osama M., and Constantine A. Axiotis. "An In-Depth Look at Leydig Cell Tumor of the Testis." *Archives of Pathology and Laboratory Medicine* 131 (2007): 311–317.

American Chemical Society. "Cisplatin." *Chemical and Engineering News Special Issue*. Available online. URL: http://pubs.acs.org/cen/coverstory/83/8325/8325cisplatin.html. Accessed April 15, 2008.

American Society of Clinical Oncology. "Profiles in Success: An Interview with Lawrence Einhorn, MD—Don't Settle for the Status Quo." *Journal of Oncology Practice* 1, 4 (2005): 167. Available online. URL: http://jop.ascopubs.org/cgi/reprint/1/4/167. Accessed August 27, 2008.

Amin, Mahul B. "Selected other Problematic Testicular and Paratesticular Lesions: Rete Testis Neoplasms and Pseudotumors, Mesothelial Lesions and Secondary Tumors." *Modern Pathology* 18 (2005): S131–145. Available online. URL: http://www.nature.com/modpathol/journal/v18/n2s/full/3800314a.html. Accessed May 27, 2008.

Atwood, Craig, and Richard L. Bowen. "Metabolic Clues Regarding the Enhanced Performance of Elite Endurance Athletes from Orchiectomy-Induced Hormonal Changes." *Medical Hypotheses* 68, 4 (2007): 735–749.

Baldwin, E. L. and N. Osheroff. "Etoposide, Topoisomerase II and Cancer." *Current Medicinal Chemistry - Anti-Cancer Agents* 5, 4 (2005): 363–372.

Ballen, Karen K., and Robert P. Hasserjian. "Case Records of the Massachusetts General Hospital. Case 15-2004: A 31-Year-Old Man with Bilateral Testicular Enlargement." *The New England Journal of Medicine* 350, 20 (2004): 2081–2087.

Brantus, Paulo V., ed. *Testicular Cancer Research Trends*. New York: Nova Biomedical Books, 2007.

Brewer, Chris. "My First Priority is Just to Live." *Testicular Cancer Resource Center*, January 17, 2007. Available online. URL: http://tcrc.acor.org/lance. html. Accessed October 9, 2007.

Canadian Medical Hall of Fame. "Dr. Charles Thomas Beer." *Canadian Medical Hall of Fame*. Available online. URL: http://cdnmedhall.org/laureates/ ?laur_id=23. Accessed May 20, 2008.

Canadian Medical Hall of Fame. "Dr. Robert Laing Noble." *Canadian Medical Hall of Fame*. Available online. URL: http://cdnmedhall.org/laureates/ ?laur_id=26. Accessed May 20, 2008.

Cancernetwork.com. *Cancer Management: A Multidisciplinary Approach*, 10th ed. *cancernetwork.com*. Available online. URL: www.cancernetwork. com/cancer-management. Accessed August 28, 2008.

Centers for Disease Control and Prevention. "DES Sons." *Centers for Disease Control and Prevention*. Available online. URL: http://www.cdc.gov/DES/ consumers/sons. Accessed August 27, 2008.

Centers for Disease Control and Prevention. "Epidemiologic Notes and Reports Testicular Cancer in Leather Workers—Fulton County, New York." *Morbidity and Mortality Weekly Report* 38, 7 (1989): 111–114.

Chemical Heritage Foundation. "Antibiotics: Dr. Hamao Umezawa." *Chemical Heritage Foundation*. Available online. URL: http://www.chemheritage. org/EducationalServices/pharm/chemo/readings/ume.htm. Accessed May 1, 2008.

Chemical Heritage Foundation. "Cancer Chemotherapy: A Chemical Needle in a Haystack." *Chemical Heritage Foundation*. Available online. URL http://www.chemheritage.org/EducationalServices/pharm/chemo/ readings/ages.htm. Accessed October 4, 2007.

Chemical Heritage Foundation. "Cisplatin: The Platinum Standard." *Chemical Heritage Foundation*. Available online. URL http://www.chemheritage. org/EducationalServices/pharm/chemo/readings/cisplat.htm. Accessed October 4, 2007.

Chemical Heritage Foundation. "Vinblastine: From Jamaica to a Cure." *Chemical Heritage Foundation*. Available online. URL: http://www.chemheritage. org/EducationalServices/pharm/chemo/readings/blastine.htm. Accessed October 4, 2007.

Clark, A. T. "The Stem Cell Identity of Testicular Cancer." *Stem Cell Reviews* 3, 1 (2007): 49–59.

Cooper, Christopher S. "Prepubertal Testicular and Paratesticular Tumors," *EMedicine.com* November 1, 2007. Available online. URL: http://www.emedicine.com/ped/topic1423.htm. Accessed August 1, 2008.

Coupland, Carol A. C., David Forman, Clair E. D. Chilvers, Gwyneth Davey, Malcolm C. Pike, and R. Tim D. Oliver. "Maternal Risk Factors for Testicular Cancer: A Population-Based Case-Control Study (UK)." *Cancer Causes and Control* 15, 3 (2004): 277–283.

Crockford, Gillian P., et al. "Genome-wide Linkage Screen for Testicular Germ Cell Tumor Susceptibility Loci." *Human Molecular Genetics* 15, 3 (2006): 443–451.

Davis, John W. "Testicular Choriocarcinoma." *EMedicine.com* March 24, 2006. Available online. URL: http://www.emedicine.com/med/topic362.htm. Accessed August 1, 2008.

Davis, John W. "Testicular Seminoma." *EMedicine.com* September 13, 2006. Available online. URL: http://www.emedicine.com/med/topic2250.htm. Accessed August 1, 2008.

Davis, R. L., and F. F. Mostofi. "Cluster of Testicular Cancer in Police Officers Exposed to Hand-Held Radar." *American Journal of Industrial Medicine* 24, 2 (1993): 231–233.

Dement, John, Lisa Pompeii, Isaac M. Lipkus, and Gregory Samsa. "Cancer Incidence Among Union Carpenters in New Jersey." *Electronic Library of Construction Occupational Safety and Health*. Available online. URL: http://www.aafp.org/afp/980215ap/junnila.html. Accessed September 27, 2007.

Donohue, J. P. "Evolution of Retroperitoneal Lymphadenectomy (RPLND) in the Management of Non-Seminomatous Testicular Cancer (NSGCT)." *Urologic Oncology* 21, 2 (2003): 129–132.

Donohue, J. P., R. S. Foster, R. G. Rowland, R. Bihrle, J. Jones, and G. Geier. "Nerve-Sparing Retroperitoneal Lymphadenectomy with Preservation of Ejaculation." *Journal of Urology* 144 (1990): 287–192.

Eble, John N., Guido Sauter, Jonathan I. Epstein, Isabell A. Sesterhenn. *Pathology and Genetics of Tumours of the Urinary System and Male Genital Organs,*

3rd ed. Lyon, France: IARC Press, 2004. Available online. URL: http://www. iarc.fr/en/Publications/PDFs-online/Cancer-Pathology-and-Genetics/ World-Health-Organization-Classification-of-Tumours. Accessed August 27, 2008.

Edes, Gordon. "Just Another Comeback Year; Adversity Can't Stop Lowell." *The Boston Globe* January 12, 2006. Available online. URL: http://www. boston.com/sports/baseball/redsox/articles/2006/01/12/just_another_ comeback_year. Accessed October 14, 2007.

Eggener, Scott E., Brett S. Carver, Davis S. Sharp, Robert J. Motzer, George J. Bosl, and Joel Sheinfeld. "Incidence of Disease Outside Modified Retro-peritoneal Lymph Node Dissection Templates in Clinical Stage I or IIA Nonseminomatous Germ Cell Testicular Cancer." *The Journal of Urology* 177, 3 (2007): 937–943.

Einhorn, Lawrence H. "Remaining Issues in Germ Cell Tumors." *Oncologist* 2, 3 (1997): 183–184. Available online. URL: http://theoncologist. alphamedpress.org/cgi/content/full/2/3/183. Accessed August 1, 2008.

Einhorn, Lawrence H. "Testicular Cancer: An Oncological Success Story." *Clinical Cancer Research* 3 (1997): 2630–2632.

Einhorn, Lawrence H. "Testicular Cancer as a Model for a Curable Neoplasm: The Richard and Hinda Rosenthal Foundation Award Lecture." *Cancer Research* 41 (1981): 3275–3280.

Einhorn, Lawrence H., and Stephen D. Williams. "Chemotherapy of Disseminated Testicular Cancer." *The Western Journal of Medicine* 131 (1979): 1–2.

Einhorn, Lawrence H., Stephen D. Williams, Amy Chamness, Mary J. Brames, Susan M. Perkins, and Rafat Abonour. "High-Dose Chemotherapy and Stem-Cell Rescue for Metastatic Germ-Cell Tumors." *The New England Journal of Medicine* 357, 4 (2007): 340–248.

Evans, Tara N., and J. Elliot Carter. "Pathologic Quiz Case: Testicular Pain and Scrotal Swelling in a 25-Year-Old Man." *Archives of Pathology and Laboratory Medicine* 128, 10 (2004): e137–e138. Available online. URL: http://arpa.allenpress.com/arpaonline/?doi=10.1043%2F15 43-2165(2004)128%3Ce137:PQCTPA%3E2.0.CO%3B2&request= get-document. Accessed May 25, 2008.

Fajen, John M., and Bruce Hills. "HHE Report No. HETA-89-126-2057, Hagaman Finishing, Hagaman, New York." *Centers for Disease Control and Prevention*. Available online. URL: http://www.cdc.gov/niosh/hhe/reports/pdfs/1989-0126-2057.pdf. Accessed August 1, 2008.

Fajen, John M., Geoffery M. Calvert and Bruce Hills. "HHE Report No. HETA-89-125-2021, Pan American Tannery, Gloversville, New York." *Centers for Disease Control and Prevention*. Available online. URL: http://www.cdc.gov/niosh/hhe/reports/pdfs/1989-0125-2021.pdf. Accessed August 1, 2008.

Feldman, Darren R., George J. Bosl, Joel Sheinfeld, and Robert Motzer. "Medical Advancement of Advanced Testicular Cancer." *Journal of the American Medical Association* 299, 6 (2008): 672–684.

FIU Magazine. "Hitting His Stride: Lowell a Success Both On and Off the Field." *FIU Magazine* Spring 2001. Available online. URL: http://www.fiu.edu/orgs/fiumag/spring_01/alumnus-profile.htm. Accessed October 14, 2007.

Fortune, J. M., and N. Osheroff. "Topoisomerase II as a Target for Anticancer Drugs: When Enzymes Stop Being Nice." *Progress in Nucelic Acid Research and Molecular Biology* 64 (2000): 221–253.

Foster, Richard, and Richard Bihrle. "Current Status of Retroperitoneal Lymph Node Dissection and Testicular Cancer: When to Operate." *Cancer Control* 9, 4 (2002): 277–283.

Freireich, Emil J. "Min Chiu Li: A Perspective in Cancer Therapy." *Clinical Cancer Research* 8 (2002): 2764–2765.

Garner, M. J., M. C. Turner, P. Ghadirian, and D. Krewski. "Epidemiology of Testicular Cancer: An Overview." *International Journal of Cancer* 116, 3 (2005): 331–339.

Geake, J., A. E. Potter, J. Lipsett, and A. Koukourou. "Stage I Seminoma in a 15-Year-Old Boy." *Australian Radiology* 51 (2007): 99–102.

Goodwin, K. D., M. A. Lewis, E. C. Long, and M. M. Georgiadis. "Crystal Structure of DNA-Bound CO(III) Bleomycin B2: Insights on Intercalation and Minor Groove Binding." *Proceedings of the National Academy of Sciences of the United States of America* 105, 13 (2008): 5052–5056.

Greene, Frederick L., David L. Page, Irvin D. Fleming, April G. Fritz, Charles M. Balch, Daniel G. Haller, and Monica Morrow, eds. *AJCC Cancer Staging Manual*, 6th ed: New York: Springer, 2002.

Guo, J., E. Pukkala, P. Kyyrönen, M. L. Lindbohm, P. Heikkilä, and T. Kauppinen. "Testicular Cancer, Occupation and Exposure to Chemical Agents Among Finnish Men in 1971–1995. *Cancer Causes and Control* 16, 2 (2005): 97–103.

Halpern, Melissa, and Ronald Jaffe. "Final Diagnosis—Large Cell Calcifying Sertoli Cell Tumor." University of Pittsburgh Department of Pathology. Available online. URL: http://path.upmc.edu/cases/case275/dx.html. Accessed May 25, 2008.

Hayes, Howard M., Robert E. Tarone, Harold W. Casey, and David L. Huxsoll. "Excess of Seminoma Observed in Vietnam Service U.S. Military Working Dogs." *Journal of the National Cancer Institute* 82, 12 (1990): 1042–1046.

Hoenig, David M., and Thomas H. Rechtschaffen. "Testicular Tumors: Nonseminomatous." *EMedicine.com* September 9, 2005. Available online. URL: http://www.emedicine.com/med/topic3232.htm. Accessed August 1, 2008.

Horwich, Alan, Janet Shipley, and Robert Huddart. "Testicular Germ-Cell Cancer." *Lancet* 367, 9512 (2006): 754–765.

Junnila, Jennifer, and Patrick Lassen. "Testicular Masses." *American Family Physician* 57, 4 (1998): 1730–1732. Available online. URL: http://www.aafp.org/afp/980215ap/junnila.html. Accessed October 4, 2007.

Kaufman, Donald S., Mansi A. Saksena, Robert H. Young, and Shahin Tabatabaei. "Case Records of the Massachusetts General Hospital. Case 6-2007: A 28-Year-Old Man with a Mass in the Testis." *The New England Journal of Medicine* 356, 8 (2007): 842–849.

Kie, Jeong Hae, Young Nyun Park, Sang Won Han, Nam Hoon Cho, and Jae Yoon Ro. "Large Cell Calcifying Sertoli Cell Tumor of the Testis." *International Journal of Surgical Pathology* 7, 2 (1999): 109–114.

Kolon, Thomas F. "Cryptorchidism." *EMedicine.com* March 8, 2006. Available online. URL: http://www.emedicine.com/med/topic2707.htm. Accessed August 1, 2008.

Kollmannsberger, Christian, Craig Nichols, and Carsten Bokemeyer. "Recent Advances in Management of Patients with Platinum-Refractory Testicular Germ Cell Tumors." *Cancer* 106, 6 (2006): 1217–1224. Available online. URL: http://www3.interscience.wiley.com/cgi-bin/fulltext/112398104/PDFSTART. Accessed October 4, 2007.

Kresge, Nicole, Robert D. Simoni, and Robert Hill. "Selman Waksman: the Father of Antibiotics." *The Journal of Biological Chemistry* 279, 7 (2004): 101–102.

Leibovitch, I., R. S. Foster, T. M. Ulbright, and J. P. Donohue. "Adult Primary Pure Teratoma of the Testis." *Cancer* 75, 9 (1995): 2244–2250.

Levin, Stephen M., Dean B. Baker, Philip J. Landrigan, Susan V. Monaghan, Eric Frumin, Mitchell Braithwaite, William Towne. "Testicular Cancer in Leather Tanners Exposed to Dimethylformamide." *Lancet* 330, 8568 (1987): 1153.

Light, Dawn. "Testicle, Malignant Tumors." *EMedicine.com* October 30, 2006. Available online. URL: http://www.emedicine.com/radio/topic680.htm. Accessed August 1, 2008.

Looijenga, Leendert H. J., and J. Wolter Oosteruis. "Pathogenesis of Testicular Germ Cell Tumors." *Reviews of Reproduction* 4 (1999): 90–100.

McGlynn, K. A., S. S. Devesa, B. I. Graubard, and P. E. Castle. "Increasing Incidence of Testicular Germ Cell Tumors Among Black Men in the United States." *Journal of Clinical Oncology* 23, 24 (2005): 5757–5761.

McGlynn, K. A., S. M. Quraishi, B. I. Graubard, J. P. Weber, M. V. Rubertone, and R. L. Erickson. "Persistent Organochlorine Pesticides and Risk of Testicular Cancer Germ Cell Tumors." *Journal of the National Cancer Institute* 100, 9: 663–671.

McLachlan, Robert, ed. "Endocrinology of the Male Reproductive System." *Endotext.com*. Available online. URL: http://endotext.com/male/index.htm. Accessed August 29, 2008.

Menweb. "Testicular Cancer. A Chat with Scott Hamilton." *Menweb.org*. Available online. URL: http://www.menweb.org/tcscotth.htm. Accessed October 15, 2007.

Meresse, Philippe, Elsa Dechaux, Claud Mommeret, and Emmanuel Bertounesque. "Etoposide: Discovery and Medicinal Chemistry." *Current Medicinal Chemistry* 11, 18 (2004): 2443–2466.

Michos A., F. Xue, and K. B. Michels. "Birth Weight and the Risk of Testicular Cancer: A Meta-Analysis." *International Journal of Cancer* 121, 5 (2007): 1123–1131.

Moraes, R. M., H. Lata, E. Bedir, M. Maqbool, and K. Cusgman. "The American Mayapple and its Potential for Podophyllotoxin Production." In: J. Janick and A. Whipkey, eds. *Trends in New Crops and Uses*. Alexandria, VA: ASHS Press, 2002. Available online. URL: http://www.hort.purdue.edu/newcrop/ncnu02/v5-527.html. Accessed August 29, 2008.

Morgan, John. "Scott Hamilton's Chemotherapy Ices Cancer." *USA Today* March 18, 2003. Available online. http://www.usatoday.com/news/health/spotlighthealth/2003-03-18-hamilton_x.htm. Accessed October 5, 2007.

Motzer, R. J., A. Amsterdam, V. Prieto, J. Sheinfeld, V. V. Murty, M. Mazumdar, G. J. Bosl, R. S. Chaganti, and V. E. Reuter. "Teratoma with Malignant Transformation: Diverse Malignant Histologies Arising in Men with Germ Cell Tumors." *Journal of Urology* 159, 1 (1998): 133–138.

MacMullan, Jackie. "Bad Bounces, Good Hands; Unflappable Lowell has been a Survivor all his Life." *The Boston Globe* January 3, 2007. Available online. URL: http://www.boston.com/sports/baseball/redsox/articles/2007/10/03/bad_bounces_good_hands. Accessed October 14, 2007.

Minichino, Adam. "Lowell Fighting Cancer Battle One Day at a Time." *OnlineAthens* July 9, 1999. Available online. URL: http://www.onlineathens.com/stories/070999/spo_0709990021.shtml. Accessed October 9, 2007.

National Cancer Institute. "Pesticide Linked to Testicular Cancer Risk." *NCI Cancer Bulletin* 5, 9 (2008): 4.

Nobelprize.org. "Selman A. Waxman, The Nobel Prize in Physiology and Medicine—Biography." *Nobelprize.org*. Available online. URL: http://nobelprize.org/nobel_prizes/medicine/laureates/1952. Accessed August 27, 2008.

O'Brien, T. R., and P. Decouflé. "Cancer Mortality Among Northern Georgia Carpet and Textile Workers." *American Journal of Industrial Medicine* 14, 1 (1988): 15–24.

Occupational Safety and Health Administration. *osha gov*. "Dimethylformamide and Testicular Cancer." *Safety and Health Information Bulletin*, February 17, 1988. Available online. URL: http://www.osha.gov/dts/hib/hib_data/hib19880217.html. Accessed May 22, 2008

Odabas, O., F. H. Dilek, H. Avanoglu, M. K. Atilla, Y. Yilmaz, and S. Aydin. "Leydig cell tumor of the testis." *Eastern Journal of Medicine* 3, 2 (1998): 78–79. Available online: URL: http://ejm.yyu.edu.tr/old/98-2/78.pdf. Accessed August 27, 2008.

Ohlson, Carl-Göran, and Lennart Hardell. "Testicular Cancer and Occupational Exposures with a Focus on Xenoestrogens in Polyvinyl Plastics." *Chemosphere* 40 (2000): 1277–1282.

Papanikolaou, Frank, and Laurence Klotz. "Orchiectomy, Radical." *EMedicine. com* January 18, 2008. Available online. URL: http://www.emedicine. com/med/topic3063.htm. Accessed August 1, 2008.

Petsco, Gregory A. "A Christmas Carol." *Genome Biology* 3, 1 (2001): Comment 1001. Available online. URL: http://genomebiology.com/2001/3/1/comment/1001. Accessed July 19, 2007.

Pettersson, Andreas, Lorenzo Richiardi, Agneta Nordenskjold, Magnus Kaijser, and Olof Akre. "Age of Surgery for Undescended Testis and Risk of Testicular Cancer." *The New England Journal of Medicine* 356, 18: 1835–1841.

Puma, Mike. "Brian's Life a Song of Friendship, Courage." *ESPN.* Available online. URL: http://espn.go.com/classic/biography/s/Piccolo_Brian.html. Accessed October 9, 2007.

Rabbani, F. H. Farivar-Mohseni, A. Leon, R. J. Motzer, G. J. Bosl, and J. Sheinfeld. "Clinical Outcome after Retroperitoneal Lymphadenectomy of Patients with Pure Testicular Teratoma." *Urology* 62, 6 (2003): 1092–1096.

Rosenberg, Barnett, Loretta Van Camp, Eugene B. Grimley, and Andrew J. Thompson. "The Inhibition of Growth or Cell Division in *Escherichia coli* by Different Ionic Species of Platinum(IV) Complexes." *The Journal of Biological Chemistry* 242, 6 (1967): 1347–1352.

Rosenberg, Barnett, Loretta Van Camp, and Thomas Krigas. "Inhibition of Cell Division in *Escherichia coli* by Electrolysis Products from a Platinum Electrode." *Nature* 205 (1965): 698–699.

Rowland, Randall G. "Role of Retroperitoneal Lymph Node Dissection in the Management of Testicular Cancer." *Cancer Control* 3, 6 (1996): 507–511. Available online. URL: http://www.moffitt.org/moffittapps/ccj/v3n6/a3.html. Accessed April 7, 2008.

Sabanegh, Edmund. "Leydig Cell Tumors." *EMedicine.com* June 11, 2008. Available online. URL: http://www.emedicine.com/med/topic1294.htm. Accessed August 1, 2008.

Samuels, Melvin L., Paul Y. Holoye, and Douglas E. Johnson. "Bleomycin Combination Chemotherapy in the Management of Testicular Neoplasia." *Cancer* 36, 2 (2006): 318–326.

Shah, M. N., S. S. Devesa, K. Zhu, and K. A. McGlynn. "Trends in Testicular Germ Cell Tumours by Ethnic Group in the United States." *International Journal of Andrology* 30, 4: 206–213; discussion 213–214.

Sheinfeld, Joel. "Mapping Studies and Modified Templates in Nonseminomatous Germ Cell Tumors." *Nature Clinical Practice Urology* 4, 2 (2007): 60–61.

Sheinfeld, J., ed. "Testicular Cancer." *Urologic Clinics of North America* 34, 2 (2007): 109–286. Available online. http://www.urologic.theclinics.com/issues/contents?issue_key=S0094-0143(07)X0021-1. Accessed September 9, 2008.

Siddik, Zahid H. "Cisplatin: Mode of Cytotoxic Action and Molecular Basis of Resistance." *Oncogene* 22 (2003): 7265–7279.

Simon, Matthew. "Jason's Story." *CBS 11 News* May 9, 2007. Available online. URL: http://www.ktva.com/cancerconnection/ci_5856578. Accessed February 5, 2008.

Sonke, G. S., S. Chang, S. S. Strom, A. M. Sweeny, J. F. Annegers, and A. J. Sigurdson. "Prenatal and Perinatal Risk Factors and Testicular Cancer: A Hospital-Based Case-Control Study." *Oncology Research* 16, 8 (2007): 383–387.

Stähelin, Hartmann F., and Albert von Wartburg. "The Chemical and Biological Route from Podophyllotoxin Glucoside to Etoposide: Ninth Cain Memorial Lecture." *Cancer Research* 51 (1991): 5–15.

Steele, Graeme S. "The Management of Nonseminomatous Testicular Cancer." *Digital Urology Journal.* Available Online. URL: http://www.duj.com/Article/Steele.html. Accessed October 4, 2008.

Steele, Graeme S., and Jerome P. Richie. "Current Role of Retroperitoneal Lymph Node Dissection in Testicular Cancer." *Oncology* 11, 5 (1997): 717–729. Available online. URL: http://www.cancernetwork.com.journals/oncology/o9705e.htm. Accessed February 1, 2008.

Takeshita, Masaru, Arthur P. Grollman, Eiichi Ohtsubo, and Hisako Ohtsubo. "Interaction of Bleomycin with DNA." *Proceedings of the National Academy of Sciences of the United States of America* 75, 12 (1978): 5983–5987.

Tasker, Fred. "A Disease that Defies the Odds." *The Miami Herald* June 13, 2002. Available online. URL: http://www.med.miami.edu/communications/som_news/index.asp?id=28. Accessed October 14, 2007.

Testicular Cancer Resource Center. "Interview with Dr. Craig Nichols." *Testicular Cancer Resource Center.* Available online. URL: http://tcrc.acor.org/iu.html. Accessed October 8, 1007.

Ulbright, Thomas M. "Germ Cell Tumors of the Gonads: A Selective Review Emphasizing Problems in Differential Diagnosis, Newly Appreciated, and Controversial Issues." *Modern Pathology* 18 (2005): S61–S79.

Waksman, Selman A., Edward Katz, and Leo C. Vining. "Nomenclature of the Actinomycins." *Proceedings of the National Academy of Sciences of the United States of America* 44, 6 (1958): 602–612.

Walsh, Thomas J., Richard W. Grady, Michael P. Porter, Daniel W. Lin, and Noel S. Weiss. "Incidence of Testicular Germ Cell Cancers in U.S. Children: SEER Program Experience 1973–2000. *Urology* 68, 2 (2006): 402–405.

Weir, Hannah K., Loraine D. Marrett, Nancy Kreiger, Gerarda A. Darlington, and Linda Sugar. "Pre-natal and Peri-natal Exposures and Risk of Testicular Germ-Cell Cancer." *International Journal of Cancer* 87, 3 (2000): 438–443.

Whitson, Jared M. "Lymph Node Dissection, Retroperitoneal." *EMedicine.com* September 14, 2007. Available online. URL: http://www.emedicine.com/med/topic3064.htm. Accessed October 9, 2007.

Wu, Hsi-Yang, and Howard M. Snyder III. "Pediatric Urologic Oncology: Bladder, Prostate, Testis." *Urologic Clinics of North America* 31 (2004): 619–627.

Young, Robert H. "A Brief History of the Pathology of the Gonads." *Modern Pathology* 18 (2005): S3–S17. Available online. URL: http://www.nature.com/modpathol/journal/v18/n2s/pdf/3800305a.pdf. Accessed October 4, 2007.

FURTHER RESOURCES

♦

Bahrami, Armita, Jae Y. Roe, and Alberto G. Ayala. "An Overview of Testicular Germ Cell Tumors." *Archives of Pathology and Laboratory Medicine* 131, 8 (2007): 1267–1280.

Bosl, George J., and Robert J. Motzer. "Testicular Germ Cell Cancer." *The New England Journal of Medicine* 337, 4 (1997): 242–253.

Campbell, Meredith F., Wein, Alan J., and Kavoussi, Louis R. *Campbell-Walsh Urology*, 9th ed. Philadelphia: Saunders, 2007.

Campbell, Neil, and Jane Reece. *Biology*, 8th ed. San Francisco: Benjamin Cummings–Pearson Education, 2005.

Einhorn, Lawrence H. "Curing Metastatic Testicular Cancer." *Proceedings of the National Academy of Sciences* 99, 7 (2002): 4592-4595.

Huyghe, E., T. Matsuda, and P. Thonneau. "Increasing Incidence of Testicular Cancer Worldwide: A Review." *The Journal of Urology* 170, 1 (2003): 5–11.

Kinkade, Scott. "Testicular Cancer." *American Family Physician* 59, 9 (1999): 2539–2544, 2549–50. Available online. URL: http://www.aafp.org/afp/990501ap/2539.html. Accessed October 4, 2007.

Netter, Frank H. *Atlas of Human Anatomy*, 2nd ed. Teterboro, N.J.: Icon Learning Systems, 1997.

Sonpavde, Guru and Lawrence H. Einhorn. "What To Do When You Discover Testicular Cancer." *Postgraduate Medicine Online* 105, 4 (1999): 229–236. Available online. URL: http://www.postgradmed.com/index.php?toc=pgm_04_1999. Accessed August 29, 2008.

Web Sites

American Cancer Society (ACS)
http://www.cancer.org

American Urological Association (AUA)
http://www.auanet.org

Cancernetwork.com
http://www.cancernetwork.com

Centers for Disease Control and Prevention (CDC)
http://cdc.gov

The Doctor's Doctor. Testes and Scrotum.
http://www.thedoctorsdoctor.com/bodysites/testis_scrotum.htm

Indiana University Simon Cancer Center, Testis Cancer Program
http://cancer.iu.edu/programs/testis

The Jason A. Struble Memorial Cancer Fund, Inc.
http://www.testicularcancer.org

The Journal of the American Medical Association Patient Page: Testicular Cancer
http://jama.ama-assn.org/cgi/reprint/299/6/718.pdf

Memorial Sloan-Kettering Cancer Center
http://www.mskcc.org/mskcc/html/44.cfm

MD Anderson Cancer Center
http://www.mdanderson.org

National Institutes of Health (NIH)
http://www.nlm.nih.gov/medlineplus/testicularcancer.html

National Cancer Institute (NCI)
http://www.cancer.gov/cancertopics/types/testicular

Sean Kimerling Testicular Cancer Foundation
http://www.seankimerling.org

The Testicular Cancer Resource Center (TCRC)
http://www.acor.org/TCRC

Washington University School of Medicine, Division of Urologic Surgery
http://www.urology.wustl.edu/PatientCare/TesticularCancer.asp

WebMD
http://www.webmd.com

INDEX

◆

A

abdomen, pain in, 33, 35
Abrams, Dan, 26
Actinomycin D. *See* dactinomycin
AFP. *See* alpha-fetoprotein
age and cancer. *See* cancer, age and;
    testicular cancer, age of onset
alpha-fetoprotein (AFP), 17, 40–41, 45, 72
American Cancer Society, 27, 31
American Urological Association, 16
antibiotics, 104
antibody, 44–45
apoptosis, 106
Armstrong, Lance, 21, 66, 88
Australopithecus, 6

B

bacteria, chemotherapy from, 104–105
B cell, 85
Beer, Charles Thomas, 104
benign tumor, 38, 82
biopsy, 17, 19
bleomycin, 99, 100, 106
blood-testis barrier, 57
blood tests, 36
blood vessels, 61
bone marrow, 107
breast tissue, enlargement of. *See*
    gynecomastia
Brian's Song, 70
Burkitt's lymphoma, 6

C

cancer
    age and, 7
    history of, 6–7

research, 8, 124
stage. *See* stages of cancer
treatment. *See* treatment for cancer
cancer staging, 89
carcinoma in situ, 123
Catharanthus roseus, 103
cells. *See also* germ cells; non-germ cells
    division, 7
Centers for Disease Control and Prevention, 111
chemotherapy
    from bacteria, 104–105
    described, 18, 87–88, 98–103, 109
    mode of action, 106
    nonresponse to, 22
    from plants, 103–104
    side effects, 107
    success of, 122
children, conceiving after treatment, 15
chorion, 41
choriocarcinoma, 65, 76–77, 81
chromosomes, 56
circulatory system and testis, 48, 61–62
cis-diamminedichloroplatinum. *See*
    cisplatin
cisplatin, 20, 24, 100–101
c-Kit (receptor molecule), 75
classic seminoma. *See* seminoma
clinical stage, 90
clinical trials, 20
complete remission (CR), 99
computed tomography (CT) scans, 19
CR. *See* complete remission
cryptorchidism, 19, 24, 110, 117–118
CT scans. *See* computed tomography
    scans
cytotoxic, 107
cytotrophoblasts, 41, 77

ABOUT THE AUTHOR

♦

KATHLEEN M. VERVILLE earned her B.S. in biology from the College of Mount Saint Vincent in 1977 and her Ph.D. in biological sciences from the University of Delaware in 1984. In 1985, she became a faculty member in the biology department at Washington College in Chestertown, Maryland, where she is an associate professor of biology. She teaches a general biology course as well as classes in microbiology, immunology, microbial ecology, and emerging pathogens. Her training, research interests, presentations, and publications are largely in the fields of environmental microbiology and science education. Dr. Verville enjoys teaching and mentoring students. In her capacity as chair of the Washington College Premedical Committee, she has worked closely for over 20 years with students interested in careers in medicine. Dr. Verville is a recipient of Washington College's Alumni Award for Distinguished Teaching. She and her husband, Frank Vella, Ph.D., also a scientist, live in Delaware. They have three grown children: Laura, Christopher, and Michael.

ABOUT THE CONSULTING EDITOR

◆

DONNA M. BOZZONE earned her B.S. in biology from Manhattan College in 1978 and her M.A. and Ph.D. in biology, from Princeton University in 1980 and 1983, respectively. She continued her education as a postdoctoral research associate at the Worcester Foundation for Experimental Biology. She joined the faculty of Saint Michael's College in 1987 where she is now professor of biology.

Dr. Bozzone's areas of specialization are in developmental and cellular biology. She teaches or has taught courses in introductory biology, science writing, cell biology, developmental biology, genetics, plant developmental physiology, and a senior seminar on the history of biology. She is the recipient of the Joanne Rathgeb Teaching Award from Saint Michael's College. An author of more than 25 publications, Dr. Bozzone is also a member of the Publication Review Panel for the *Journal of College Science Teaching* and an ad hoc reviewer for *American Biology Teacher.* An enthusiast for science education at all levels, Dr. Bozzone designs laboratory teaching materials for students in high school and college, and also works with students who are training to become biology teachers. She and her husband, Douglas Green, who is also a biology professor at Saint Michael's, live in Vermont with their two teenage daughters.